A FREE SPIRIT
Dialogue with Margaret Anna Cusack The Nun of Kenmare

PADDY MCMAHON

Copyright © 2016 Paddy McMahon

www.paddymcmahon.com

All rights reserved.

ISBN-10: 1530564670
ISBN-13: 978-1530564675

CONTENTS

INTRODUCTION	1
CHAPTER: I	5
CHAPTER: II	7
CHAPTER: III	8
CHAPTER: IV	10
CHAPTER: V	15
CHAPTER: VI	18
CHAPTER: VII	20
CHAPTER: VIII	21
CHAPTER: IX	22
CHAPTER: X	23
CHAPTER: XI	25
CHAPTER: XII	28
CHAPTER: XIII	31
CHAPTER: XIV	36
CHAPTER: XV	41
CHAPTER: XVI	45
CHAPTER: XVII	51
CHAPTER: XVIII	58
CHAPTER: XIX	61
CHAPTER: XX	64
CHAPTER: XXI	65
CHAPTER: XXII	70
CHAPTER: XXIII	74
CHAPTER: XXIV	76
CHAPTER: XXV	81
CHAPTER: XXVI	83
CHAPTER: XXVII	85
CHAPTER: XXVIII	87
CHAPTER: XXIX	89
CHAPTER: XXX	91
CHAPTER: XXXI	93
CHAPTER: XXXII	95
ABOUT THE AUTHOR	97

INTRODUCTION

Early in 1978 I began to receive communications - for want of a better word - from what I understood were spirit guides or guardian angels. I had always been comfortable with the notion of a guardian angel, but I hadn't given any thought to the possibility of communicating with them.

At that time I had been working in the Civil Service in Dublin. From an early age I had been interested in writing. I dabbled in poetry, short stories, including children's stories, plays, even a novel. In 1978 I got an idea to try a film script about Daniel O'Connell, a major Irish historical figure of the late 18th to mid - 19th centuries. I researched whatever material I could find. One day I mentioned my project to an acquaintance who happened to be a manager of a branch of the Bank of Ireland. He told me that there was an impressive looking biography of O'Connell in the Bank's HQ. (It seemed to me to be a strange resting-place for it until I discovered that O'Connell had founded the National Bank, which was later absorbed into the Bank of Ireland.) Through his good offices I got a loan of the book which was (is) a beautifully bound volume written by Margaret F. Cusack and entitled The Liberator: His Life and Times, Political, Social and Religious.

Margaret Cusack had been internationally famous as the Nun of Kenmare. She was born in 1829 in Dublin. She was brought up as a member of the Anglican Church. In her teens she moved to England with her mother. Later she fell in love with a young man named Charles Holmes. They became engaged to be married. During a visit to Ireland she got the sad news that Charles had died suddenly. She was devastated for a number of months afterwards. Perhaps motivated by her loss she turned to intensive religious searching which led her to become an Anglican nun. About five years later, in 1858, she converted to Roman Catholicism. A year later she entered a Poor Clare convent in Newry, County Down, in Ireland.

Her given birth name was Margaret Anna Cusack. When she entered the Poor Clares she took the name Sister M. Francis Clare.

She moved to Kenmare in County Kerry in 1861 to help found a convent there. She wrote prolifically and her books had a wide international circulation with the proceeds from them going to the support of the Poor Clares and their work amongst the poor.

She was actively interested in political and social reform and particularly in getting equal rights for women, with education as a special priority. She also founded a Famine Relief Fund in 1879. She is reputed to have saved thousands of men, women and children from dying of starvation. The Nun of Kenmare established herself as a powerful champion of justice and equality. Predictably she incurred the disapproval of the Bishop of Kerry. She left Kenmare in 1881.

After more difficulties with Church authorities in Ireland, Margaret moved to England where she established the Order of Sisters of St. Joseph of Peace, with the objective of choosing works for peace which would provide benefit especially for the poor.

Because of shortage of funds the Bishop of Nottingham, in whose diocese her order was based, asked her to go to the United States for help. She set sail for America in October 1884. Her reputation as a world famous author and political activist had preceded her and she encountered much episcopal disfavour and lack of cooperation. However, despite severe ill health, her indomitable spirit prevailed and a convent was opened in Jersey City in March 1885.

For the next three years she worked tirelessly to further the aims of her new order. Time and again she met with rejection from her ecclesiastical superiors. Eventually in 1888 she decided that the interests of her community would be best served by her leaving it, which she did. Her personal integrity couldn't allow her to remain as a member of a Church with such inflexible patriarchal structures and in 1889 she was received into the Episcopalian Church and reverted to a large extent to the Anglican beliefs of her early life. Her autobiography (The Nun of Kenmare: An Autobiography) was published, also in 1889. She travelled widely throughout the United States speaking to large audiences.

At the end of 1891 she decided to go back to England. Despite her increasingly failing health she continued to write. She died on 5th June 1899 in Leamington, England.

Back in 1978 when I read her book about Daniel O'Connell I had never come across anything about Margaret Cusack. I didn't even know that she had ever existed. I kept getting a message, purportedly coming from her, that she was one of my guides. I had no way of proving that physically, obviously. It seemed that the real reason for me being led to the book was to be introduced to her. I accepted that she was one of my guides and over subsequent years I had many proofs, which were convincing as far as I was concerned, of the help coming from her.

Between 1981 and 1996 I wrote a series of five books, entitled THE GRAND DESIGN: Reflections of a soul/oversoul, in collaboration with a spirit being known to me as SHEBAKA. During that time I understood that I was also in constant communication with Margaret in connection with other areas of my life.

Earlier this year (1998) I had written and published a little book of excerpts from the five volumes of THE GRAND DESIGN. I was looking through some papers when a newspaper feature about Margaret Cusack, which was written in 1987 and which I had retained although forgotten, literally jumped out at me. At the same time I was receiving a strong message that she wanted to collaborate with me in writing a book. So here it is.

She used the initials MFC in correspondence. I have prefaced her contributions accordingly.

Margaret Anna Cusack was a remarkable woman by any standards. In having the honour of collaborating with her I'm expressing my admiration and respect for her as an outstanding pioneering spirit to whom the world owes much.

So often we play down our potential - "What difference can I make? I'm only one person." In her life on earth Margaret Cusack presented us with an inspirational example of the significant impact one person can make on global consciousness. And she's obviously not resting on her laurels.

In writing my other books I dropped my surname, which is Mc Mahon. I'm doing the same with this book - just in case there's any presumption that I might have a split personality!

The book is in a form of continuing dialogue spread over a number of days. I have deliberately not tried to categorise each day's dialogue under chapter headings.

Paddy McMahon
January 1999

Note: The book "There Are No Goodbyes / Guided By Angels" contains extracts from this book.

I
17 July 1998

MFC: After a lapse of nearly one hundred years in physical time since I took leave of the planet I might be expected to have mellowed - and I have, I have. I used up a lot of energy in fighting injustice as I saw it and I often regarded myself as a victim of injustice. But the boundaries of conservatism are never easily breached and those souls who are brave enough or foolhardy enough to try tend to be isolated. Certainly I who was Margaret Anna Cusack was effectively sidelined - though never silenced, I'm glad to say!

It's often said that there's no proof of life after death because nobody ever comes back to tell their relatives, friends, or interested researchers, about their "new life". Many souls have returned, and continue to do so, in a reincarnational context but usually they don't remember their previous existences - which doesn't help from a proof point of view. But many others have been communicating through the centuries with those humans who are open to receiving them. So I can't take any credit in projecting, as it were, a voice from the grave.

You thought I looked very grim in photographs you have seen. Well, I wasn't grim. Sometimes I was short-tempered and impatient and wanted very much to get my own way. I liked to be the one to give the orders, so that obedience didn't come easily to me. But I liked to laugh and I did have a good sense of humour.

Still, I took life far too seriously. I was too much of a crusader for my own good - some might say for the good of others, particularly those who had to put up with me. I can say with certainty that I'll never be canonised - unlike some others with whom I'm in close contact!

What are we going to write about? There won't be any preaching, I promise you. I'd like to talk about my own experience since I moved on. I'll probably not be able to resist the temptation to provide some social commentary to do with how I see the planet now.

II
18 July

MFC: Never mind about your beloved Shebaka. You're not going to lose your connection with him by working on this project with me. Anyway I've always been in daily contact with you even when you were in the thick of The Grand Design books. You made a deal with me, too, and I'm collecting!

Looking back on my life as Margaret Anna Cusack and Sister/Mother Francis Clare, I see it as a mish-mash of idealism more or less constantly in conflict with implacable authoritarianism. I would see what I firmly believed was needed and I was impatient to meet the needs. Ultimately I, the originator of many projects, became the biggest obstacle to their being implemented.

I'm greatly honoured by the outpouring of love in my direction from many fine people. I bless them all.

III
20 July

PF: *How do I know that I'm not fooling myself in thinking that the soul who was known as Margaret Cusack is communicating with me in this way? Wouldn't it be a grave injustice to her if I was to record material purporting to come from her without being certain that that's in fact so? But how can I be certain? Is looking for certainty a lack of trust on my part? I don't know. It's one thing accepting that she has been in regular communication with me as a guide; that only affects myself. It's another thing to expect other people to accept the validity of the communications without some proof. So where do I go from here?*

MFC: As you well know, there's no way of providing absolute proof which would be acceptable to all and sundry. You've been over all this sort of territory many times in your explorations with Shebaka - and with me, too. So let's forget about all that and get on with the project.

"Margaret Anna Cusack fell asleep June 5th, 1899: aged seventy years." That's what my friends put on my coffin. The thought was nice. I said goodbye to my poor old body, which had been tired out for a long time. It had struggled with ill-health for many years and had lasted a lot longer than I could reasonably have expected.

I experienced a lot of confusion in the immediate aftermath of my transition. Why does that surprise you? I had been a Protestant, a Roman Catholic and again a Protestant. I had been engaged in polemics both in speech and in writing for much of my life. I wanted to change the way things were run and particularly to help the underprivileged, the vast majority of whom were women. Since I was in religious life I was expected to be obedient to my ecclesiastical superiors, most of whom were authoritarian old men. To them I was a nuisance, somebody who didn't know her place. I had great plans -

so I thought - which I could only partially, or not at all, implement because of the purple brick wall fencing me in. I wasn't wanted by my adopted Church and yet I was vilified because of my leaving it. It seemed as if I had created conflict where I wanted harmony and hate where I wanted love.

When I found myself free of my body and I was no longer confined by physical disability I wasn't sure how I'd be received in my new state. After all, I had become accustomed to rejection. What if God turned out to be like the figures of authority I had known – His representatives, as they believed?

IV
21 July

PF: *If it's okay with you I'd like our communications to be conducted as a form of dialogue rather than a straightforward discourse from you.*

MFC: You mean you don't want to let me loose! I'd prefer dialogue – I was never one for lectures. I'll get to say whatever I want to say anyway. Remember you chose me as a guide!

PF: *I don't remember but I'll take your word for it. You were saying that you were in a state of confusion after you passed on. How did that dissipate?*

MFC: I looked on as my friends lovingly dealt with my body and said nice things about me and even mourned my departure, although I had been a burden to them. While I felt alive and vigorous, which was something I hadn't experienced for a long time, I also felt sad.

PF: *My understanding is that there's a guide or a loved relative or some form of welcoming committee ready to greet souls when they move on. What happened in your case?*

MFC: I was very much on my own – an interested observer, if you like, - while the funeral arrangements were going on.

After the ceremonies were all over I suddenly became aware of what I can only describe as a radiant being smiling at me and then giving me a big hug. I think you have an impression that I was a severe, untouchable sort of person when I was on earth. I had a sharp tongue sometimes, but I was very soft-hearted really and I loved demonstrations of affection. So the hug was great. We had instant rapport and communication. I was greatly relieved. My state of confusion slipped away and I knew I was home.

PF: *Is it off putting for you when I interrupt our sessions and go off and do something else?*

MFC: It isn't. I'm constantly on a wavelength with you anyway. That's my job, you might say – or part of the job I took on. I have a lot of other irons in the fire, as I'm sure you'd expect, but I can tune in to you whenever I want or you want. As you know, there are others, too, in your network apart from Shebaka and my (humble!) self.

I wasn't aware of any movement but I suddenly seemed to be a guest of honour at a big party, with hordes of wonderfully loving beings hugging me and kissing me and giving me the most amazing welcome. What a celebration! I knew them all. It was a reunion. I can't describe the feeling of joy. It was literally like nothing on earth.

PF: *Having lived such an intensely religious life, did you expect to be judged and perhaps punished for your "sins"?*

MFC: I'm not sure that I'd agree with you about the intensely religious bit. I certainly lived intensely and I was in religious life for a long time, so maybe you can put the two together.

Of course, my conditioning was that I'd be summoned before a judgement seat of some kind and called to account, if not by God Himself, by some of His inner circle. My thinking was influenced by hierarchical configurations, inevitably male dominated. However, I was so infused with the joy of the reunion that all thoughts of judgement went out of my head.

PF: *How did you know all the others at the reunion and how did they know you? What did you look like?*

MFC: I just knew them. They were all like effulgent beings of light, yet easily distinguishable one from another.

PF: *Was there a gender distinction?*

MFC: There was and there wasn't. I know that's a strange sort of answer. The best way I can try to explain it is that there was a transcendence of gender like, say, when you communicate on a soul level with somebody. Yet there were some whom I had known as female and some as male and I seemed to continue to communicate with them in that way, and they with me.

PF: *Maybe I shouldn't be asking a nun – or an ex-nun - this, but was there any sexual frisson?*

MFC: I wasn't always a nun. Mind you, nuns in my day weren't allowed – or didn't allow themselves to entertain what might be labelled as impure thoughts. Anything to do with sex would have been decidedly impure! Yes, there was sexual frisson, as you put it, in the sense of a wonderfully joyful intimacy which is what sexuality involves, as I understand it.

PF: *I just want to check with you at this stage whether I'm receiving you as you would wish. Is there anything you'd like to suggest that would enable easier communication?*

MFC: It's fine. You continue at your own pace. If you're sluggish – which you are sometimes! – I'll hold off and there won't be any flow. You get the signs.

PF: *Thanks. That's a relief to me. What happened next?*

MFC: You're asking that question, of course, from your perspective in your linear time frame. I could say that nothing happened and everything happened. I was no longer aware of time. I was getting used to feeling completely free. On earth I was always busy – things to be done, ideas to be explored, books to be written, bishops to be cajoled. Now here I was with no agenda, but full of the joy of just being, and surrounded by kindred spirits in every sense of the word.

To help you understand; the reunion went on for maybe a few hours or a few days in your time. I hadn't yet shaken off completely the feelings of illness and tiredness which were my constant companions for so long on earth. At some stage one of my old/new friends suggested that I might like to take a little rest. I agreed, and instantly I seemed to be lying on a wonderfully comfortable bed in a beautifully appointed room with soft music enveloping me. I relaxed into the harmony of it all and I suppose you might say that I fell into a deep sleep. It's misleading to talk of things happening in sequence because everything seemed to be happening all at once.

In any event the relaxation process refreshed me and once again I found myself with a group of the friends I had met earlier. We had a lot of catching up to do.

> **PF**: *Weren't you beginning to be curious about what you were going to be doing? I can't imagine you being happy sitting around relaxing and doing nothing, no matter how enjoyable the company.*

MFC: I didn't have to do anything but I wasn't doing nothing, if you can understand that. Impressions were coming to me all the time. Even as I thought about something – for example, how my Sisters were getting on – I found I was able to get a picture – or maybe a vision would be better way to describe it – of that immediately. It was all completely effortless. Suppose you want to visit your friends in America. You have to go through a lengthy process of booking tickets, paying fares, hours of travel interspersed with waits at airports. None of that for me. The only drawback was that I couldn't talk to my darlings or touch them. Well, I could talk to them but they wouldn't hear me. Initially that was a big disappointment, particularly as I had had to suffer the pain of separation from them while I was still bodily on earth. After awhile I adjusted to the way things were and began to enjoy helping out in unobtrusive ways.

> **PF**: *As Margaret Anna Cusack, and then perhaps more particularly as Sister/Mother Francis Clare, you would have built up a relationship with God as a Supreme Being in some form. As time passed, in a manner of speaking, where did God fit into your picture?*

MFC: For a start there was still no sign of any call to judgement, and I began to realise that there wouldn't be. There wasn't any indication of God wanting to see me for any other reason either, which was both a relief and a disappointment.

V
22 July

PF: *I'm sorry for stopping yesterday when you had only begun to answer my question.*

MFC: Stop when you will. It doesn't bother me.
 I was in continuing contact with many souls who were involved in lots of activities depending on their individual preferences. It may interest you to know that you were there, too, having completed one incarnation and coming to terms with the idea of your present one. It was during that interval that we agreed that I would act as one of your guides. But I'm digressing.

PF: *Sorry for interrupting again. I would appreciate it very much if you could find a way to come through to me more obviously. It's a bit like being on a faint telephone line at present and I want to be sure that I'm recording accurately what you're transmitting to me.*

MFC: There's no rush. We can go as slowly as suits you. In that way your mental processes are free to be more still. I'm coming through more clearly now, am I?

PF: *Yes. Thanks.*

MFC: Thank you. Where was I? God, yes. I was releasing the mental restrictions that were built up in my physical lifetime – having, of course, already released the material ones. Impressions came flooding back to me of what I had previously known, including the notion of God not as a separate being at all, but as the life force in all of us – along the lines of the information conveyed through you by Shebaka in the Grand Design books. There was to be no judgement other than that which I chose to make on myself.

PF: *What you're saying is that you knew all that before you were born into your life as Margaret Cusack?*

MFC: Yes.

PF: *Why, then, didn't you carry that knowledge with you? Wouldn't it have made life much easier for you? Also, wasn't it misleading to be a representative in a significant way, admittedly sometimes rebellious, of organisations which promulgated a concept of God which you knew to be mistaken?*

MFC: As I found out to my cost in my jousts with the windmills of authoritarian institutions and their autocratic representatives, the wheels of change grind slowly. My aim was to be an agent of change, a reformer. It was necessary that I should go into an environment and be part of it before I could seek to transform it. I had to have a passion for what I was doing. I couldn't be an outsider. Where there was injustice I needed to be a victim of it. Where there were sadnesses and griefs and lonelinesses I needed to experience them all. I needed to be human in ever sense of what that meant at that stage in human evolution. I also needed to be female because human evolution would remain stagnant unless it could be rescued by a balancing of male and female consciousness within individuals primarily and then globally as a consequence. When souls choose to incarnate or reincarnate there's not only the physical restriction but also the mental one – or, I should say, the consciousness one. If I wasn't part of that restriction, if I didn't understand it and identify with it and also feel it, I couldn't have negotiated with it passionately.

PF: *But if your truth as you knew it in your non-physical state perceived God, and consequently all life, in an immeasurably more expansive and unlimited way than you expressed it on earth wasn't your choice of human manifestation an unfair compromise in so far as you yourself and also those whom you sought to help were concerned?*

MFC: In the context of the nineteenth century my priority was to try to create a climate of improved conditions for people, particularly those who had unequal rights and opportunities, such as women and the poor, who, of course, included both sexes. I felt that my role was to be a launching pad from which others could orbit. I sought to be a pragmatist more than a philosopher – or perhaps to be a pragmatic philosopher! Perceptions of God could wait. In any case they would be as individual as souls, and would continue to be. We could explore the higher reaches of spiritual expression when people were more comfortable in their living conditions as well as in their self-esteem.

VI
23 July

PF: *When you looked back at your life as Margaret did you feel that you had achieved what you set out to achieve?*

MFC: Strangely enough, I did. In my later years on earth I didn't have much of a sense of achievement. I had written a lot and talked a lot. I had raised a considerable amount of money to help people in need. I had served in as loving a way as I could. But I had also been a source of dissension, many of my projects collapsed, I was often disillusioned, I see-sawed between religions. At the end, very much alone except for a few stalwart friends, I couldn't see myself as other than a failure, well intentioned though I was.

In spirit, though, there was – there always is – a very different perspective. It's a futile and altogether pointless exercise trying to judge a life's expression within its time span. When I looked at that earth life from the much broader vantage point of spirit I saw that through my writings, my talks, my contacts with people, the ideas I put into motion, my passion for equal opportunities for everybody, I had opened doors to the raising of consciousness outside of the limits of a particular time scale. In other words, I had made a contribution the effects of which would live on after I passed on. Once I had taken that on board in spirit I was able to forgive myself for all the human failings I had manifested and let myself enjoy the freedom I now had.

PF: *Given that you've had other incarnations besides the Margaret Cusack one and that you have in a larger context moved on from her into more expansive spirit expression, why are we having this dialogue, which I presume you would like to see published?*

MFC: There's an upsurge of interest in Margaret at present as you have recently found out. Her importance as a pioneering spirit will be emphasised. (I'm talking about her now in the third person so that you'll understand that I'm not on an ego trip; whatever recognition she gets is of no relevance to me in an individualistic sense as I now am, but it is highly relevant and significant in so far as it helps to raise people's consciousness.)

Why? Because the public climate is more favourable than it ever was towards this sort of experimentation. There's a big push on from the spirit side to use whatever broadcasting stations are open to us. What else would I be doing?! Are you interested in what I have to say?

PF: *Yes. Very.*

MFC: Others will be, too. Margaret worked at breaking down barriers so why wouldn't I, the 'ascended' Margaret!, continue to do that – especially when I have a willing transmitter?

PF: *At this stage do you want to outline in more detail particular topics you want to explore?*

MFC: I want to shout a big YES to life, to the death of death, if I may put it like that, so that anybody and everybody can say – 'I know my body is going to die, but I know, too, that there's nothing to fear in that – it's a celebration of continuing transformation in life.' I want to go into more detail about how I express myself in my present state and about what life in spirit, generally, is like. People may be interested to know how souls in spirit continue to interact with humans. As I said already, I don't think I'll be able to resist giving suggestions as to how, in my view, things might be better managed on earth. And I'll be glad to answer any questions you may have.

VII
24 July

PF: *What do you want to discuss today?*

MFC: I was deeply in love with Charles Holmes and he with me. My future was firmly set in a particular direction. When he died I was devastated. Yet, had he lived, there wouldn't have been a Sister/Mother Francis Clare. Of course I have met Charles since and we have resumed our relationship. We love each other in a more complete way than would have been possible on earth. Needless to say, Charles was close to me while I was going through all my travails on earth. He hasn't reincarnated; neither of us will do so again. You might say that these communications are a sort of reincarnation!

PF: *Many people don't believe in reincarnation and of course, it's not comprehended by the Christian tradition, at least since the sixth century. You obviously take it for granted.*

MFC: Yes. When I was last on earth it wasn't something that impinged on my consciousness. I was more concerned with existing conditions and how to fix them there and then. But it's a fact of life. I know – I've done it many times.

VIII
25 July

PF: *Apologies again for having interrupted you yesterday.*

MFC: I'm not controlled by time like you. So please don't apologise any more. It's easy for me to pick up where I left off. I don't have any memory lapses. I have no need of memory now – there's nothing I need to forget so I can forego the protective screen of memory.

Many of the recorded communications from spirit have come from souls with exotic sounding names – like your friend (and mine) Shebaka. I don't mean to take away from them in any way – far from it – but some people might relate more easily to someone with a homely name like Margaret Cusack. It's ordinary, like everyman or everywoman.

IX
26 July

PF: *Yesterday was a rather blank day for me, I wasn't receiving you well so I had to call a halt.*

MFC: I won't seek to come through unless I see that conditions are right for you. If you're too tired, as you were yesterday, I'll just keep quiet.

I want to give you an idea of what I get up to.

Nobody tells me – or anybody else here – what to do. It's important to say that, because people often have an impression of a type of ruling hierarchy in spirit who assign missions to their minions. You can forget all about hierarchical structures in spirit. There are enough of them on earth to be going on with. We have what you might call a co-operative system. We can't sit idly by, so to speak, while people struggle. There are hordes and hordes of souls in spirit engaged in all sorts of schemes designed to help their brothers and sisters on earth. We have conferences and we set up committees. We choose the ways in which we'd like to help, bearing in mind the areas that most suit us. We may decide to appoint a co-ordinator who will keep an overview of our different programmes and, of course, we meet frequently to discuss how we're progressing. While we're very aware of human traumas and the suffering that many of our human "charges" are experiencing, and we certainly don't take them lightly, nevertheless, because we can see the bigger picture, we retain our feelings of joy and are in what I might describe as states of concerned detachment. We wouldn't be much help to anybody if we got caught up emotionally in every passing crisis.

X
27 July

MFC: In any event, what humans see as crises aren't crises at all. O, I know I had my own share of crises when I was on earth and then when I was going through them I wouldn't have thanked the me that I am now for making statements like my first one this morning. However, as you know, when people look back they often wonder how they had got so worked up over situations that later on seem so trivial. From our perspective on the mountain top, as it were, we see the purpose behind the happenings and we rejoice in the understanding that sometimes comes later on and are so grateful when we can help people to reach that understanding.

We have great fun here. Don't let anybody think for a minute that we're clones of each other. We're able to express our different and unique personalities in ways that we didn't feel free to on earth. And I think you can gather from the tone of my communications, even though you're putting them into rather careful language, that I'm anything but a pietistic, antiseptic type of individual.

However, it would be misleading of me to present a picture of life in spirit as full of uninterrupted joy. It is for many, according to their states of awareness. But, unfortunately, there are still many souls in spirit who are experiencing what I can only call the tortures of hell, except that, mercifully, we know that it's only a temporary hell. The duration of it is determined by how willing they are to open themselves to a new awareness of themselves.

How do they get into such a state? I'll give you an example.

A man, I'll call him Johann, was born into a well-to-do family in Austria in the early part of this, the twentieth century. He qualified as a doctor and went to work and live in Germany. His move to Germany coincided with the Nazi developments. He was an idealistic young man who saw his medical career as a vocation rather than a job. He couldn't but be aware of the changing political scenario, but he was so absorbed in his work that, to some extent, it passed him by; until, that is, he was drawn into it.

He was given a commission in the German army, which initially was quite pleasing to him in that he saw himself as having opportunities to give whatever healing he could to wounded soldiers. However, he wasn't allowed to stay in that role for long. His new assignment was to examine imprisoned Jews in order to select those of them who, in his opinion, were fit for manual work. You know the fate of the rejects, those considered unfit by him. His instructions were clear - selection or rejection - and beyond that he didn't know in the early stages what happened as a result of his decisions. It was inevitable, of course, that he found out. He was horrified. He went to his superior officer and requested that he be transferred to another post where he could fulfil his medical vocation. He got an unambiguously direct answer - 'Go back to your post or you'll be shot as a traitor.' After much agonising he went back and tried to convince himself that he was doing his patriotic duty, that maybe the authorities had access to information that he didn't, which indicated that Jews were in some sinister ways seeking to undermine the stability of the State. He became as efficient a robot as he could.

The years went by, the war eventually ended and the extent of the Nazi atrocities began to be revealed to the world. Johann could no longer anaesthetise himself. He sought oblivion and committed suicide. There was no oblivion, of course. He couldn't get away from himself. The realisation that he couldn't destroy himself, that he had no choice but to live with himself indefinitely, was the source of the most agonising mental torture for him, a despair that knew no relief.

One of the tasks I took on was to help Johann to come to a stage where he could even begin to accept, if not to love, himself. As you can imagine, it wasn't an easy task.

XI
4 August

MFC: The first and most important part of my task was to help Johann to unburden himself. He was racked with guilt. In his view of himself he was utterly worthless. He felt that he had completely reneged on his vocation and betrayed his profession through his cowardice in saving his own life at the cost of many others. In the early stages of our contact he couldn't even acknowledge me. I kept turning up, sitting silently near him, projecting love at him, just being with him.

After some time he began to look at me somewhat furtively. Eventually he asked me what did I want. I said - 'nothing.' That was the end of our conversation then. We continued to sit silently together.

I didn't stay with him continuously - I kept coming and going, so that he had long periods by himself. I noticed that, in spite of his resistance, he couldn't disguise his pleasure when I turned up. He was slowly beginning to enjoy contact with someone else, who was obviously not looking at him with abhorrence, which was how he was feeling about himself.

When I felt that the time was right I told him that I was with him as a representative of divine love, and that I wanted to help him forgive himself and enjoy being alive and well. 'How can I forgive myself?' he asked in torment. 'You don't know all the terrible crimes I have committed, all the suffering I have caused.' "Yes, I do. I know everything", I replied. After a long pause he asked - 'And yet you don't reject me?' I assured him that he was now in a dimension where he would meet no rejection. Haltingly he began to talk, to let all his self-recrimination pour out. And I listened.

PF *When you say 'he began to talk' I presume it wasn't talking in* *the sense of using a language and sound as we do on earth?*

MFC: Languages as you know them are unnecessary in spirit. We function through thought transmission. The nearest equivalent in your terms may be an automatic translation service. For example, somebody at an international gathering is speaking in his native language and his listeners through their ear pieces are receiving him in their own languages. Another example would be somebody who works as a medium easily receiving messages from souls in spirit although that would not have been possible because of language difficulties if they were all on earth. In our communications I'm not using any words - I'm transmitting thoughts to you and you're interpreting them into your own words.

PF: *It's probably pointless, then, to go to the trouble of learning a lot of languages while on earth.*

MFC: It depends on how much access one wants to other cultures. As the barriers between the spirit and physical worlds are being broken down language distinctions will become more and more irrelevant.

PF: *Will we use words? Read books? Life without books would seem very barren to me.*

MFC: There will always be writers and books and readers. Suppose you go into a bookshop where there are books in many different languages. If you open a book which is, say, written in Swedish it will be incomprehensible to you because you have no knowledge of Swedish. Imagine, though, that you have reached a stage that when you open the Swedish book you automatically understand the words although you have never studied the language. It's hard to grasp from where you're sitting.

PF: *It's not so difficult for me because I'm used to communicating with spirit beings like yourself and Shebaka and others, and, as you said, the process of communication transcends language in that we don't seem to use words. What bothers me is that in the progress of evolution a form of telepathy will take over which will eliminate the* *need for words altogether.*

MFC: We can operate at whatever level we wish. Those who like to use words will continue to do so. It's not an either/or situation. Limitation of possibilities only applies to your present human thinking. There's no need to try looking around corners that don't exist. There's nothing to stop you having the best of all worlds.

PF: *I diverted you from Johann.*

MFC: I let him talk away. I could see him observing me, wondering was I horrified by what he was telling me. As he saw that there was no change in the way I was relating to him he became more expansive and there were even occasional glints of humour.

Gradually things evolved to the stage where he was agreeable to let me take him to meet other souls, who accepted him unquestioningly. He began to allow himself to enjoy their company spontaneously. I no longer have to come and get him, so to speak. He automatically connects with the group, or with one or more of them, as he wishes.

PF: *What about the victims of his selections? Will he have to face them?*

MFC: He may wish to. There's no hurry. Sooner or later it will happen - as it does on earth.

PF: *How do you mean - 'as it does on earth'?*

MFC: People don't realise - mercifully - that they're in frequent, often daily, contact with some who have abused them in one form or another in a previous life or previous lives. The reverse is also true - they may be in contact with victims of abuse by them. It's never all one way traffic. Johann may eventually choose to reincarnate into an environment where he will have opportunities to make restitution in some form to one or more of his victims and, through them, to humanity as a whole. That will be his choice. Opportunities other than reincarnation will also be available to him. The main thing is that he's on his way.

XII
5 August

PF: *Are there many souls continuing to exist in states of depression/withdrawal?*

MFC: Many indeed, unfortunately. In Johann's case it could be said that he was an abuser through force of circumstances. While the effects of his decisions were far-reaching for many people he acted under duress without any trace of malice. His true loving nature was cloaked by his unwillingness to put his ideals above his own safety. A common enough example of human frailty, would you agree? - dramatised, of course, by the scale of the operations in which he was involved.

Many people perform acts of horrific abuse and show no trace of remorse. Their way of life is totally based on their needs for self-gratification irrespective of how that can be achieved. Any concept of soul or spirituality is alien to them. They get vicarious enjoyment from exercising power over others and seeing others suffer.

I have been dealing with somebody like that. Let's say his name was Alfredo. On earth he was a vicious criminal. He was head of a notorious gang who terrorised people. He was an active participant in every conceivable form of human degradation. He showed no mercy and no regard for life. Increasing age didn't mellow him - rather the reverse. Up to the day he died he was issuing orders with ruinous effects for helpless people.

When he shed his body Alfredo was lost. He no longer had all the trappings of power that he relished. There was no point in his shouting for his lackeys - which he did endlessly. He was beside them, behind them, in front of them, but they couldn't hear him. You can imagine his frustration and all the threats of the most dire punishments he poured out at them, but they just ignored him. He was discovering that he was helpless and to say that he didn't like it would be a somewhat large understatement!

It might be said, understandably, that he deserved to be left like that indefinitely given all the suffering he caused during his earth life. Things don't work like that in spirit, though. As I've said already, there's no judgement. Souls punish themselves through their states of mind, as Alfredo was now doing. I was there to help him but there wasn't anything I could do in an immediate sense except be patient.

An important point to mention here is that I didn't feel in any way superior to Alfredo. I was in a different dimension of awareness and therefore in a position to help him whenever he would be ready to receive help, and I understood that how Alfredo expressed himself in his earth life did not reflect his soul essence; his exercise of his free will had temporarily obscured it completely. My job was to help him to see that.

He was so obsessed with what was going on with his gang and his own fury at being unable to get through to any of them that it was impossible for me to achieve any communication with him for what would be a long time in your terms - several years. I tried various means, such as bringing along relatives of his - parents, a grandmother whom he had loved as a child, others - but nothing worked. But we who act as guides never give up. We know that there's inevitably going to be a breakthrough. With unconditional love there has to be. And in Alfredo's case there was eventually.

When Alfredo was a child he had a playmate, a little girl - I'll call her Lucilla - roughly the same age as himself. They lived near each other and they played together regularly. Sadly for Alfredo she died when she was only seven. The grandmother whom he had loved was also dead at that stage and there was nobody else in his world that he felt close to.

Lucilla, of course, was no longer a little girl, but we arranged that she would appear to Alfredo as he knew her. We had to choose our opportunity carefully because his obsessiveness with what was going on with his former 'empire' had created what in your terms I might call an impenetrable brick wall around him. But sooner or later he was going to let his defences down, if only for an instant. We snatched such a moment and he became aware of Lucilla, a little girl just as she was so many years earlier.

PF: *How was it possible for her to appear like that?*

MFC: No bother at all. In spirit we can take on any appearance we like. All we need to do is imagine it. People try to do that on earth, too, through plastic surgery and different hairstyles, and even putting on new faces every day with makeup - but you wouldn't know anything about that, of course!

PF: *I find it a bit disturbing that souls can put on different forms from one second to the next. I'd be on tenterhooks wondering to whom I was relating.*

MFC: No, you wouldn't really. The form is always consistent with our persona or our style so that we have no difficulty in recognising each other. You might understand more easily if you see it like an actor playing different roles on stage with appropriate makeup and costumes. The actor is still the same person.

The central point here is that Alfredo wouldn't have known Lucilla in any other form.

In any event, the transformation in Alfredo was remarkable. Briefly he became a child again. They held hands and they danced and they laughed. All the intervening turbulence fell away from him. Until he remembered and he went behind his wall again. But a start had been made and gradually the wall came down and Lucilla's love triumphed. There's a long way to go with Alfredo yet. It may take many centuries in your time, but once the barrier is down the rest will follow.

In Alfredo's case I have had no direct involvement with him. I acted as an orchestrator behind the scenes. We often work that way. The outcome is what's important – not who achieves it.

XIII
6 August

PF: *That's also how you sometimes work with people whom you guide, isn't it?*

MFC: Yes, of course. As above, so below, so to speak. If we can't get through directly we find another way, for example, by seeking the help of somebody close to our "charge" – somebody who would be more receptive to our prompting.

PF: *Having a 'direct line' isn't all that important, then?*

MFC: In the long run, no. It can even be a hindrance if people set up an anxiety in themselves because they don't seem to be getting any obvious answers. Trust first, then leave the hows open. I'm presupposing, of course, that there's an acceptance that guides never fail those whom they've agreed to guide.

I'd like to give you another example of how I operate.

When she was on earth Monica grew up in a deeply religious environment. From an early age there was never the slightest hint of a doubt in her mind but that she would be a nun. In due course she entered a convent and subjected herself with total dedication to all the disciplines of religious life. She was an exemplary nun. She welcomed every assignment, no matter how tedious. She willingly volunteered for extra duties. She punished herself rigorously if she thought that she had transgressed even the most minor regulations.

She was an obvious candidate for higher office and in the fullness of rime she became the Superior of her Order. In her discharge of her office she was as severe with others as she was with herself. The rules were sacrosanct. The service of God allowed for no laxity.

Demonstrations of affection were taboo. Monica's God had no time for smiles or hugs. She was respected and feared. Nobody got close to her. She showed no vulnerability. She was an excellent administrator and believed that that was how she showed her love.

When the time came for Monica to hand over the reins of office to somebody else she did so willingly, in accordance with the will of God, as she believed totally. She lived into her eighties and died with all the comforts of religion secure in the belief that she was going to her due reward in Heaven for her faithful service on earth.

Monica observed the funeral ceremonies and listened to the tributes paid to her. There were no tears, there was no sadness because of her departure. The whole affair was full of solemnity. It was all just as it should be, in Monica's view.

I had chosen to help Monica through her transition. Any approach which held even a hint of levity would be inappropriate. It would never have done if I appeared as a nun dressed in a mini skirt and wearing a stud in my nose, or something like that. I decided that for Monica I'd lay on all the style. She had lived her life in a spirit of total self-denial and service. She had fulfilled her side of a bargain with God, as she saw it, and there could be only one reward – Heaven. So Heaven was what she found – that is, my presentation of Heaven, as I viewed Monica's perception of it. I laid on a solemn religious ceremony with a phalanx of officiating dignitaries dressed in splendid ecclesiastical robes. A centrepiece of the ceremony was a special welcome for Monica. She was very pleased.

Next I arranged that she would be introduced to members of her Order who were now in spirit and who tended to see life in much the same way as she did.

> **PF**: *Why did you choose to lay on a type of theatrical production for her which might be said to be leading her up the garden path?*

MFC: She was already dealing with the transition from physical to spirit life and leaving behind all the securities she had known within the confines of her Order. I felt that she needed to have the comfort of the fulfilment of her expectations until she was ready to open her mind to other possibilities. That was the sort of welcome she expected and that's what she got. The mind creates its own reality. I was simply acting as an agent of her mind until she could let go of its rigidity. She was happy within her perception of happiness.

PF: *Wouldn't she be as well off staying like that indefinitely – happy, as you said?*

MFC: I said that she was happy within her perception of happiness.

The main snag was that she had suppressed the joy in her, the essence of her divine nature. My job, as I saw it, was to help her to open herself to that joy, that love. I did so gradually by appearing to her in my angelic paraphernalia – which I can tell you are very impressive! I took her to all sorts of gatherings – discussion groups where often weighty topics were explored with much humour and laughter, dances, theatrical performances, concerts, all sorts of happenings, a feature of which was joyful expressiveness. She was a bit resistant at first, but she couldn't get past the status my angelic appearance gave me and she gradually relaxed and began to enjoy herself. Slowly she let go of her rigidity and accepted that it was permissible for her to indulge herself in what would have previously seemed to her as perilously close to devilish temptations.

PF: *I presume you haven't introduced her to the notion of reincarnation yet?*

MFC: No, not for a while yet. She needs to be free of her old patterns, particularly to understand that it's okay to enjoy herself, before I go that far. She was always so busy and felt guilty if she wasn't, that it's very enjoyable for me to see her getting used to doing nothing and coming to the realisation that she's not expected to do anything, or put any pressure on herself in case by being idle she was neglecting her duty. There will be plenty of opportunities for her to serve if she still wants to, as I'm sure she will. Service with a smile!

PF: *Are there some people who don't have any hang-ups at all when they pass on?*

MFC: Yes, increasingly so. They're not always that easily recognisable when they're on earth because they don't fit into any pietistic mould or what might be seen as a model of sanctity. If I were to single out a particular feature or characteristic of them it's their open-mindness. Dogmatism is no-no for anybody wishing to experience fully the joy of transition – and I don't mean that in an exclusively religious sense; intolerance in any form fits neatly into its wide embrace.

> **PF**: *This may not be a fair question to ask you as the founder of an order of nuns which is very much alive and well. Is the practice of religion likely to be a hindrance or a help towards experiencing the joy you mentioned?*

MFC: It's a question that I'd have had to come to sooner or later anyway.

It would be strange now if I gave you a dogmatic answer, wouldn't it? I'd be hoist on my own petard, in a manner of speaking.

Religion is only a tool. It's neither good nor bad – it all depends on how people use it. For many it's a stepping stone, an introduction to spirituality. People have problems if it becomes the be all and end all of spirituality. The more it loses its harshness and rigidity and allows love to take over the better.

> **PF**: *That's a diplomatic sort of answer.*

MFC: Sincere, though.

> **PF**: *I don't doubt that. If you had your life as Margaret over again would you have founded your Sisters of St Joseph of Peace Order?*

MFC: Yes.

> **PF**: *No qualification?*

MFC: None. I'm proud of them all, what they are, what they have done and are doing. I have always kept in contact with them – less obsessively since I've lost my bossiness.

> **PF**: *It's hard for me to imagine a state of being where not alone there's no time as such but also no need of sleep or rest. For example, you could continue this type of communication indefinitely but I can't because I get tired. Do you ever get bored or restless? Or you know how we humans often need the hope of being able to look forward to tomorrow. You have no tomorrows or yesterdays. Do you ever need to have something to look forward to? For instance getting this book finished and published?*

MFC: I understand. Wouldn't you prefer, though, if you didn't get tired?

> **PF**: *Surely.*

MFC: Believe me, I knew what it was to be tired and ill. There was so much I wanted to do and I couldn't.

Boredom results from restriction of creative expression. I have no such restriction.

As regards looking forward – I can if I want to. I can play that sort of game. You mention this book specifically. I know it has to be written at your pace and I'm happy with that. I know it will be published and I'm happy about that, too; I say 'will be' rather than 'is' because it has to fit into your linear time scale.

Now I see you need a break:

> **PF**: *Yes.*

XIV
7 July

MFC: I'd like to dwell a little further on the question of looking forward. It's a truism to say that you can't live in the future any more than you can live in the past. That's why one can say that in real terms there's only the present. If you live in a state of continuing expectancy about the future – you know the 'I can't wait for such and such to happen' syndrome – you're diminishing your prospects of being able to enjoy the present and you're also creating a pressure around how you're going to respond to future events when they become your present. All the same, you wouldn't be human if, when you know that there's something coming up which you feel you're going to love, you didn't allow a warm glow in yourself about it. You're sending that glow before you, so to speak, and it's preparing the way for your continuing enjoyment of life.

It's important to say, though, that if you're feeling completely miserable about your life as it is and you're looking to some person or event to change that for you, you're likely to be disappointed because how you respond to your present is how you're creating your future. That may seem like a hard reality, but it's a recognition of the power of each soul in the exercise of free will. Humans have generally very little concept of the power of their thoughts, positive or negative.

> **PF**: *The fact is that we humans are stuck with a linear time structure. We carry the effects of our past into our present and to the extent that we allow our present to be affected, if not controlled, by those effects we're predetermining our future patterns, or our continuing present, if you like. I understand all that but what I still find difficult to grasp is how you operate. Is your present a much wider field than ours? Does it encompass what we might call our future?*

MFC: In other words, can I see your past and your future all rolled into your present? And can I see my own past and my future in my present? Are these the questions you're asking?

PF: *Yes.*

MFC: I could be clever and say to you that I have no past and no future and neither have you. But you know that today is Friday and tomorrow is Saturday, the next day is Sunday, this is the month of August, next month is September, and so on. You can't avoid planning ahead, at least to some extent, for tomorrow, next week, next month, next year. I also do forward planning. For example, I prepared strategies in dealing with Johann, Alfredo and Monica. They were loose strategies which could be adjusted spontaneously. I couldn't foresee exactly how they were going to react, although it wasn't difficult to make fairly accurate predictions.
People are often very confused about this whole area, which includes the world of predictions.

PF: *I have to pause for a few minutes because I'm beginning to speculate and to analyse. I want to be still so that I don't try to put words in your mouth.*

MFC: We're back on the air! Don't worry – if you go astray I'll give you a nudge.

To answer your first question – I can see your past and your future rolled into your present. What was your past in linear terms is obviously clear like history – but recorded more accurately than your histories often are. What will be your future is not so clear in detail although in broad outline it is. Put in an ultimate setting, we all know where we're going – to complete release of our self-imposed separation from our divine natures. How we get there is influenced by how we exercise our free will.

Because we agreed that I would act as one of your guides, with your permission I have access to all the details of your evolution, as well as to your overall objectives in reincarnating into your present life. I can see how you have progressed and are progressing in fulfilling what you set out to achieve. In so far as you're staying with your broad plan I can reasonably expect that you will continue to do so, and therefore I can say with some confidence that I can predict what you would call your future. However, if you decide, or to the extent that you decide, to change course, I'll have to change my predictions. I can't interfere with free will, but I can see the patterns in how people exercise their free will and it's not too difficult to foresee what's ahead of them, if I may put it like that.

PF: *I take it that you're talking particularly from the perspective of a guide?*

MFC: Yes. A soul in spirit who might not be familiar with all the details of a person's evolution or that person's life purpose could easily allow its own controlling tendencies to take over in giving advice. It might genuinely think that it had the person's best interests at heart and the person might give the advice more weight, or see it as infallible, because it's coming from a spirit source.

At the same time, I don't want to convey an impression that souls in spirit, who are not acting within an agreed arrangement as guides, don't give helpful guidance. I know that they often do. All I'm saying is that it may be a bit hit and miss. As long as people see it that way and preserve their own power of discrimination, that's fine.

To turn to the second question – can I see my own past and my future in my present? The simple answer is I can, with the proviso that I allow myself complete freedom to respond spontaneously to whatever comes up and to express myself in whatever way I wish without any inhibition or restriction. In other words, I am as I am and, in your terms, I know I will be as I am. Do you understand that?

PF: *I don't know. Up to a point I do – I think!*

MFC: It's hard to imagine being out of time when you're in time. Maybe we've gone as far as we can go with it.

PF: *When you talk about freedom – is there no authority figure at all that you have to obey? Are there no rules or laws that prescribe* *even in broad terms how what I might call celestial societies should function?*

MFC: I had to put up with enough authority figures in my Margaret life to last me for eternity. No, there's no authority figure at all. Complete and utter freedom. Most people aren't ready for freedom. They seek security in being told what to do or how to be. That's how autocrats and institutions get their power.

One of the biggest challenges facing souls is to learn how to be free. Monica is a good example of that.

PF: *I think it may be difficult for many humans to accept that there's no regulatory system at all in spirit.*

MFC: There is to the extent that souls, including those temporarily in human form, are being helped to find freedom in themselves. The free spirits, as it were, come together to set up ways of helping those who aren't yet free. It's as simple as that. It's divine love operating through all souls. There can be no boss since we're all equal in God – or in our divine essence, if you prefer. Some are temporarily at higher levels of awareness than others. That may make them appear to be superior beings, but they know they are not, nor would they want to be. Their objective is to heal rather than increase the suffering which has been, and continues to be, caused by some seeking to take precedence over others.

PF: *Suppose you yourself need help whom do you consult? Or do the answers you need come to you automatically?*

MFC: As I mentioned earlier, we tend to operate in groups or committees – if we wish to do so, of course. We have lots of discussions. We're always available to each other. I don't really need help. I don't mean to sound arrogantly self-sufficient, but since you've asked the question I'm answering it as honestly as I can. I don't have any material needs. I exist spontaneously and I can do so in ways that would be difficult for humans because of all the restrictions with which they have to cope. You see, souls need help while they're still separated from their divinity.

Separation = helplessness.

> **PF**: *The idea of unity with divinity, with a Source, or God, may perhaps bring up a fear of loss of individuality. Is there any basis for such a fear?*

MFC: None at all. Unity means a totally free flow of divine energy within each soul and enables each soul to be fully itself in every way.

> **PF**: *Suppose you decide that you're tired of being a guide. Maybe you become a bit fed up because souls, both in human form and in spirit, don't seem to be getting anywhere no matter how much you try to help them.*

MFC: You're asking me to suppose something that couldn't happen. I don't get tired, as I've already said, and I don't get fed up, either. It's easy for me because I don't exist within limitation. And I know that there's always a way to achieve a breakthrough, as with Alfredo. I can wait, you see – I don't have a deadline, if you'll excuse the pun!

At some stage I may discontinue acting as a guide in the way that I do at present. Eventually I will anyway because no one will need my help.

> **PF**: *That's a long way off, I'm sure.*

MFC: Yes indeed, unfortunately.

> **PF**: *You've said you don't need any help. But are there dimensions of which you have little or no knowledge?*

MFC: There are myriads of projects, dimensions of experience, etc., that hold no interest for me. I only delve into whatever interests me. I can find out about other matters if somebody asks me, or if I want to, at any particular stage. Let's say I know where to get my answers whenever I need them. I don't carry all the knowledge of the universe around in my head, if that's what you're asking. I can consult my celestial internet whenever I like! I can be as deliberately ignorant or deliberately knowledgeable as I want to be. Freedom!

XV
8 August

PF: *Here on earth we tend to look for a place of our own where we can have out own personal possessions and lifestyle – such as a house or an apartment. Do you have anything like that?*

MFC: Your residences are solid structures which are usually fixed in one place and are not transportable. We can create any type of building we like just by imagining it. And if after awhile we don't like what we've got – we may wish to transform it or have something totally different – we can have instant manifestation according to our wishes. Many souls who have been house proud on earth find to their great joy that they can have exact replicas of what they left behind just by thinking about them. Or keen gardeners can, as it were, transport their gardens (not physically, of course,) to their new surroundings. These are not flimsy cardboard cut out structures. They're just as 'real' as yours, although that's difficult for you to conceptualise.

The same thing applies to food and drink; we can have the experience of them in whatever way we wish, once we realise that we can.

PF: *Are there some who don't so realise?*

MFC: Yes – particularly those who can't or won't let go of earth, who resent finding themselves in a new state. Some of the most pathetic examples are those who were serious users – or, I suppose I should say, abusers – of alcohol and had lived much of their lives in public houses or such like, and continue to hang around their old haunts; or those who were so attached to their houses and their possessions that they can't bear to tear themselves away from them; or those who had built their lives around their businesses and couldn't believe that others would be capable of managing them, so they must stay on to keep an eye on them; or, generally, those who were trapped by obsessiveness. Sooner or later, of course, we find ways to prise them loose.

While on earth souls use a density of form, including their bodies. In the non-physical world they continue to use form which is just as real, though not dense, as the physical.

> **PF**: *A big difference, then, between life in spirit and life on earth is that the soul in spirit can have the house or houses, etc., that suits its style at any given time, whereas the poor human can only have all that if he/she has enough money.*

MFC: You can throw in, too, that the soul in spirit doesn't have to cope with ageing or physical illness or disability of any kind. It seems a bit unfair, doesn't?

> **PF**: *Just a bit!*

MFC: Remember, though, that souls choose to incarnate of reincarnate into the physical world. There's no compulsion whatever on them to do so. As you know, their choice is influenced by their need to free themselves from patterns which they had established during previous earth experiences. The quickest way to do that is likely to be by re-entering similar types of environment which would confront them with those patterns.

I wouldn't like to give an impression that life on earth is intended to be a very serious, gloomy sort of ironing out experience. I know that that has been a common view of it, but happily it's changing.

> **PF**: *Apart from money, I suppose that the most central driving force on earth is sex. How about that?*

MFC: We've touched on that subject briefly already.

How could it be that something to which so much energy is devoted on earth would not feature powerfully in spirit? Money is in a different category from sex; while it is, of course, a form of energy or exchange of energy, it's external to people, something they use, like furniture or washing machines. Sex, on the other hand is a deeply intimate form of communication between people. We know that it's commercialised and abused, but that doesn't take away from its beauty in its ideal usage.

As you have often seen, what happens on earth is that, as they expand their awareness, people are no longer satisfied with sexual relations, per se; rather, they're looking for soul mates with whom they can enjoy sexual intimacy as a special form of communication, a profoundly spiritual experience. It happens that people don't meet soul mates in a particular lifetime or, if they do, circumstances prevent them getting together. The resultant loneliness and longing can be devastating for some; others are happy with special friendships which don't have sexual overtones.

The good news is that all souls have soul mates and they find them sooner or later and get together with them in a total sharing, which includes sexual intimacy if they so wish.

PF: *Souls in spirit don't have babies, do they?*

MFC: Don't I keep telling you that everything is possible in spirit? The whole panoply of earth was set up from spirit. All your miracles are engineered in spirit. There are no new souls, just souls taking on different forms. Thus with your babies. So, of course, babies can be born in spirit if souls so wish. Souls can even experience all the joys (!) of childbirth if they want to do so. Just bear in mind that anything that's possible on earth is countless times more easily achievable in spirit.

PF: *So a woman who, say, suffered deep disappointment in not having her longing for a baby satisfied can look forward to having her dream realised in*
spirit?

MFC: Indeed she can.

XVI
10 August

PF: *Is it fair to deduce from what you said in our last session that you're not in favour of celibacy?*

MFC: Prescribed celibacy, no. If people are voluntarily celibate that's how they're expressing their free will. Anything that's imposed is contrary to the way of spirit.

PF: *Some people may not want to be celibate but don't have any opportunity to be otherwise.*

MFC: There could be all sorts of reasons for that. It's probable that it's in accordance with their soul purpose. For example, they may feel that they had indulged themselves obsessively in sexual activity in previous lives and want to balance the scales.

Let me tell you another story.

We're back in the sixteenth century during the reign of King Henry V111 in England. A young man named Stephen has set his heart on becoming a priest but he's in a dilemma because in spite of himself he has fallen in love. Her name is Catherine. She returns his love. After much agonising he decides that Catherine has come into his life as a test of the strength of his vocation and that what's required of him is to sacrifice his human love for the greater glory of God.

Although she's heartbroken Catherine can only accept his decision.

Stephen is duly ordained as a priest and settles into his duties.

Martin Luther is assuming a public profile and what became known as the Reformation is getting under way. King Henry, initially, and his

Chancellor, Sir Thomas More, are defenders of the then established Church with the Pope as its head. There's much toing and froing of arguments and diatribes. None of all this is of any immediate concern to Stephen. There's no radio or television to keep him informed of what's going on. He gets on with his work as best he can.

In the meantime a marriage has been arranged for Catherine by her parents. She hasn't forgotten Stephen, but she adapts herself as wholeheartedly as she can to her life as it's now unfolding.

Time passes. One day Stephen is called urgently to the bedside of a dying woman. To his horror he finds that it's Catherine whom he hasn't seen, and has tried to forget, for many years. She's still conscious. All the feeling that both of them had tried to suppress comes to the surface. He has to remind himself to give her the last rites. She dies holding his hand.

Stephen rails against the cruel fate, as he sees it, that forced him to make a choice between his vocation and Catherine. He tells himself that if he had married her she would never have got the infection that took her still young life.

In due course he hears about the religious developments. Those who are following Luther's line are regarded as heretics and are liable to be tortured or put to death by burning if they don't recant. Stephen is now in a rebellious frame of mind and open to the new teaching. He becomes part of an underground network aiming to spread the new 'gospel'. Unfortunately for him spies are everywhere and he's exposed. He's severely tortured and eventually recants. A broken and disillusioned man, his health fails and he dies a few short years later.

The scene shifts to Ireland in the nineteenth century. It's a time of hope, much of it inspired by the Liberator, Daniel O'Connell. A young couple, Ruairi and Maureen, childhood sweethearts, are due to get married. Then comes the Great Famine to blight all their crops and their hopes. There's a place for one of them to go to the land of opportunity, America. After much persuasion from Ruairi Maureen agrees to go first with Ruairi to follow later whenever he'd get a chance to do so. Heartbreak once again as Maureen leaves. Hope turns to despair for Ruairi as blight follows blight, starvation takes its toll and he becomes one of the many fatal victims of the Famine.

Maureen survives and after many hardships becomes a teacher. She helps many children of those Irish emigrants who managed to negotiate the journey to America and all the vicissitudes of settling into a new culture. Eventually she gives up hope of meeting Ruairi again. She doesn't marry, although that's not for want of offers. Much respected, she dies some thirty years after leaving Ireland.

Now we come to the present century. Robert is a psychiatrist living in the United States of America. He was married with two children, but now, in his mid-50s, is divorced. He has recently taken on a new client, a twice married and divorced woman named Freda. She was born in Ireland but has lived in America for the past forty years – her parents had emigrated when she was only five. She has one daughter by her first marriage and two sons by her second. She is now a grandmother. For the past seven months she has been living with a man who is pressing her to marry him, but after two failed marriages she's hesitant about accepting his proposals. She's also not sure about her feelings for him.

After a few sessions with Freda Robert is in an ethical dilemma. He realises that he has fallen in love with her. While he has been increasingly looking forward to his meetings with her, he decides that he has no choice but to discontinue seeing her and to refer her to a colleague.

Freda, too, had been struggling with her feelings for Robert. She tells herself that this is par for the course with him, that she's just one of many women who imagine that they're in love with him, and she resolves that she won't fall into that trap. She has been coming to the conclusion that maybe it would be better if she stopped seeing him when he tells her that he's calling a halt to their sessions. She's very disappointed but at the same time relieved. She doesn't want to have any more emotional turmoil in her life and, in her view, she would certainly be putting herself in the way of it by continuing to see him.

Time passes and they both get on with their lives. She's still in her

relationship but refusing to commit herself to marriage. He has had a brief affair which ended by mutual consent.
One day he's passing a bookshop when he gets an urge to go in. He's arguing with himself that he has no time at present to indulge his love for books, but still he responds to the urge.

Inside the bookshop he suddenly comes face to face with Freda. Their pleasure at seeing each other is spontaneous. Even though he realises that he's going to be late for an appointment he invites her to have coffee with him. She accepts. They enjoy each other's company enormously.

I hardly need to fill you in on the rest of the story. It is love realised and fulfilled. Released from the burden of being her therapist he is able to be himself in all his humanity. She in turn sees that to him she's an attractive woman rather than a client. They literally fall into each other's arms, and I can say in true romantic parlance that they live happily ever after.

You have gathered, of course, that what I've been outlining are episodes from the evolutionary journeys of two souls. In human terms the first two episodes have tragic outcomes while the third one ends happily.

I wanted to tell you this story partly because I'm an (old?) romantic at heart, but mainly to show how free will and conditioning intertwine with and often interfere with and block the flow of love. Stephen was caught within the cage of his rigid beliefs. In the case of Ruairi and Maureen they were physically separated because of their decision – although primarily Ruairi's – that Maureen should go ahead of him to America – which was an understandable decision in the circumstances. When they again appeared as Freda and Robert their coming together was delayed until relatively late in their lives. But love found a way in the end to clear all the hurdles.

A sceptic might say that it was just a coincidence that Robert happened to get the urge to go into the bookshop at the very time that Freda was there – but it wasn't. We're always on the lookout for such opportunities. People often ignore our nudges but we never give up.

It's important to say that on their separate journeys both souls will have been seeking to resolve other aspects of their evolutionary debits, including the karmic effects accruing to other relationships.

Ruairi punished himself for his rejection as Stephen of Catherine and sought to compensate by ensuring that Maureen – the 'resurrected' Catherine – would have at least an opportunity for survival and freedom from hardship.

In the third episode Robert could again have been caught in a vocational trap, as he had been in the first (as Stephen).

> **PF**: *Third time lucky!*

MFC: Except that luck didn't enter into it.

> **PF**: *I notice that in each of the episodes they were in the same gender relationships. Is that usual?*

MFC: That was their choice. It's always up to the souls themselves how they want to act out their evolution.

> **PF**: *You would have been seen as a feminist before that term came into vogue, and perhaps you would still be regarded as such. Does that mean that you had a preference for female incarnations?*

MFC: I was a feminist, if you wish to call me that, because something needed to be done about the oppression of women. The uniqueness of each soul, no greater or lesser, needed to be reflected in human manifestation so that the planet earth would be better able to fulfil its purpose as a vehicle for growth in awareness. That couldn't happen while one gender assumed a dominant position over the other. The same thing applies to racial inequalities or, indeed, any form of discrimination. So, yes, I was a feminist because that was what was needed. I'd have been a masculinist if that was what was required at the time! Now I'm both or neither.

It's nice for people that there are separate genders. One balances the other and, ideally, they're not in competition with each other. They're just vehicles for different means of expression.

XVII
11 August

MFC: I want to refer back briefly to our dialogue yesterday.

I would wish that the fragment of the evolution of two souls which I outlined would be seen as a message of hope. Maybe things don't work out in one lifetime, but they will in another.

> **PF**: *The trouble is that with all our advances in technology, etc., we want 'quick fixes'. From my own experience I know that people don't like to be told that they might have to wait a year or two for something they want to happen – let alone a lifetime or two or three!*

MFC: I was a prime example of impatience in action myself. Many people, admittedly inadvertently, tried to teach me patience by withholding their approval of my plans; but I wasn't very responsive so the lessons kept being repeated over and over. I was full of how much I wanted to get done and how little time I might have, particularly because of my ill health. Later I realised that it was enough for me to sow seeds. Others would be there to reap the harvest.

I'm using myself as an example because I want people to know that, although my life on earth as Margaret was sprayed with disillusionment and rejections, now I'm as happy as can be. Everybody deserves to be happy – and so they will be.

> **PF**: *Were you ever tempted to reincarnate as a man – maybe so that you could become a bishop or a cardinal or a pope, even?*

MFC: That would have destroyed my image as the Nun of Kenmare! No, it seemed best that I stay put.

PF: For many years you were regarded as an unmentionable – probably even worse than a heretic – in Roman Catholic circles because of your decision to revert to Protestantism. No doubt it was more or less an article of faith that you had condemned yourself to eternal damnation. Did you have any fears yourself that you might have done so?

MFC: I did have some fears, as I mentioned at the outset of our dialogue. Not so much of eternal damnation and certainly not because I had left the Roman Catholic church. The fears were more to do with my sense of failure in connection with what I had set out to achieve. It was very painful for me to leave my Sisters in the Order I had founded and cherished. That was a huge burden of grief for me for the rest of my life. I carried them in my heart. I was turning away from the authoritarian Church, but never from them.

PF: For a long time even you own Order didn't acknowledge you – acting under orders, I know. Did that hurt you?

MFC: In my human state, yes. Later the only thing that mattered was that the process I had initiated really flowered after I left. My notoriety had become a big stumbling block in the way of expansion of the Order and, more important, its work. I could see the bigger picture which took care of any traces of egotism I might have carried with me.

PF: I meant to ask you earlier when you were talking about how souls in spirit can have whatever they want – like houses, gardens, etc. – what about you? Do you have a place of your own, if I may put it like that?

MFC: I knew you were thinking about that earlier, but I deliberately generalised your question. It's not that I didn't want to answer it but I thought it was more important to paint the general picture for you before dwelling on my personal situation.

There's a gradualism that operates in spirit as well as on earth. It's to do with expansion of consciousness or awareness. At one stage in my evolution I'd have accepted the having of a house or apartment of my choice as a more or less fixed reality, like I would have similarly on earth. But as my awareness expanded I became more and more open to the true nature of reality – which is that I'm continually creating it from within myself. In other words, there's nothing stagnant or fixed where I'm concerned.

During my adulthood in my last life on earth – as Margaret – my home was a moveable feast. I never really had a place that I could call my own. In the long run that was an advantage for me – and I want to stress that I'm only talking about myself here – because I wasn't married to any particular building or locality – although there were times when I'd like to have been.

> **PF**: *I accept that you've said that you're only referring to yourself, but would you say that it's a disadvantage for people to become very attached to, say, a house or an apartment or a garden?*

MFC: It depends on the level of attachment. If people are obsessive about their 'places' that's likely to slow down their progress in spirit. As I've already explained, some just hang around as what you call earthbound spirits; others become as obsessed with their spirit houses, etc., as they were with their earthly ones. Obsessiveness in any form is to be avoided as far as possible if a soul's journey towards increased awareness is not to be sidetracked.

> **PF**: *So are you saying that you don't have any particular home now?*

MFC: Please bear with me while I explore this question further with you. Suppose you had the freedom to be instantly wherever you imagine you'd like to be, by yourself or with whomever you'd wish to be, to be out in the open or ensconced in the most comfortable surroundings you could ever wish for, would you confine yourself to one fixed setting? In your present environment or circumstances if you say 'no' you might regard yourself as taking an easy way of escaping from your responsibilities, or creating difficulties for yourself by having to adapt to different cultures, including methods of entertainment, such as television programmes. But suppose you have no responsibilities. Yes, you want to help others, but you're not going to be of any use to them if you get all caught up in their troubles. The best way you can help them is to guide them towards taking responsibility for themselves. You're in a position to do that. There are no different cultures since that's a feature of life on earth only – at least at the level of awareness you have reached. You can see any television programme you want, if you're still interested.

Now, may I put the question to you again – in that scenario would you confine yourself to one setting?

PF: *No.*

MFC: That's my answer. I don't mean to imply that what suits me would suit others, any others. What I'm talking about is being free, free to be, from which follows freedom to do what ever one chooses to do. Being free in myself means that I allow that freedom to each and every soul, which in turn means that there's no question of trying to control any of them. Freedom also means loving. Once I'm free in myself I'm free to love unconditionally – I will only attach conditions to my loving if I'm feeling confined or insecure in myself.

PF: *How different are you now from how you were when you were last on earth – as Margaret?*

MFC: You know how sometimes in horse racing blinkers are put on a horse to prevent it from looking sideways – it can only see straight ahead. That's a rough analogy but it's accurate enough. I was blinkered when I was on earth – deliberately so, in order that I could fulfil my purpose there – like the racehorse. I could only see what was directly in front of me and my concentration was focused on that. When I moved back to life in spirit, after I had adjusted to it I could see how my role slotted into the panorama of evolution – the grand design, if you like.

I'm very different and I'm not different at all – seemingly contradictory statements, but yet true. Each soul has basic qualities – or perhaps style would be a better description – which are constant although often partially or nearly totally obscured. The big difference now is that I'm free, with all that that means. I obviously wasn't free while I was on earth.

> **PF**: *Before I fell asleep last night I asked you to arrange, if it suited you, that I meet you while my body was sleeping and that I'd remember the meeting this morning. I was looking for reassurance (replaying my usual record) that all this isn't a delusion of a fragmented mind (mine). How can I ever know for sure while I'm in my body? When I'm out of my body, while it's asleep, surely I could get proof, if only I could remember?*
>
> *Anyway I was disappointed when I woke up this morning to find that I had no memory of any meeting.*

MFC: You have been consciously communicating with me now for twenty years. You have acknowledged that you've had lots of proof during that time. Why all this fuss now?

> **PF**: *Because it's different now. We're going public – or, I should say, I'm going public because you won't be coming out from behind the veil!*
>
> *I know we've discussed this early on in our dialogue and I'm sorry for bringing it up again. Why wasn't it possible for you to arrange a meeting?*

MFC: But we're meeting every day. It wouldn't be any different. We often meet in groups and separately while your body is sleeping. You carry through whatever you need from the meetings into your physical state. Are you aware of me now as you're writing?

> **PF**: *Yes.*

MFC: How?

> **PF**: *I can feel your presence and I can vaguely see you – more clearly when I close my eyes. I can't make out any features but I can see a sort of outline. When I say that I can feel your presence it's like a very warm energy around me, often as if you're looking over my right shoulder. You seem to be wearing your nun's habit – I presume that's*

in the interests of identification.

Because I've seen photographs of you, though, I could be projecting one of them onto my "screen", as it were.

MFC: Even if you could remember our nocturnal meetings you'd still be arguing with yourself as to whether they were 'real' or 'imaginary'. Isn't that so?

You wouldn't be going to all the trouble of sitting down laboriously writing and typing with one finger after your fashion unless you felt that our communication was genuine. Twenty one years ago you hadn't even heard of Margaret Anna Cusack. Historically, she belonged to the nineteenth century. Why bother with her now? She's not such a prominent historical figure that you could be accused of delusions of grandeur in going public about your association with her. It would hardly be generally seen as a major scoop to be receiving daily communications from a dead nun, albeit a rebellious ex-nun, would it?

PF: *All that doesn't bother me. I don't mind so much about deluding myself as long as I don't delude anybody else.*

MFC: Do you feel that you're deluding yourself?

PF: *No.*

MFC: So then you're acting in good faith. It will be up to people reading our dialogue to decide for themselves how they react to it. Is there anything in my communications that doesn't jell with you?

PF: *No.*

MFC: Then we may as well keep going.

PF: *Yes. I forget sometimes how much I rely on trust in my life and how it's never misplaced when I don't put conditions on it.*

How do you think the Sisters of St. Joseph of Peace will react to the idea of their founder being involved in this sort of stuff which is still beyond the pale as far as their Church is concerned?

MFC: They shouldn't be surprised. I was a controversial figure as Sister/Mother Francis Clare. Why would I be different now? I was never one to be silenced. I'm speaking to them and to any others who are open to hearing me with a message of encouragement, hope, and, above all, love. That's a continuing legacy from me. In all humility I can say that I'm a conduit of divine love, of which there's an inexhaustible supply. My Sisters are way ahead of the institutional Church and have been constantly open to the need to take risks in their thinking and their actions.

PF: *Have you any special message for them now?*

MFC: Other than that I love and applaud them, no. Each succeeding generation has brought its own dynamism. I'm very grateful that they're no longer ashamed of me! They are idealistic, caring and loving, and are making a big contribution towards peace and harmony on earth.

XVIII
16 August

PF: *You mentioned earlier that you'd like to discuss how souls in spirit continue to interact with people. You have already gone into that to some extent, but perhaps you may have some additional comments.*

MFC: As we've seen, there are different levels of contact. Guides, for example, have agreements with those whom they guide and are always instantly available to them; the contact is more sporadic where other souls are concerned.

The following story may be helpful as an example of continuing interaction between the two states.

Jane is a woman in her thirties, happily married, with three children, aged six, four and two. The household revolves around her. She looks after all the details of the domestic scene with superb efficiency.

She had launched a promising career as an interior designer, but she has put it on hold until the children are older. Her husband, Oliver, is a partner is a busy firm of accountants. Life is moving along smoothly and harmoniously for the family.

Jane has never suffered from other than minor illnesses, such as colds. When she begins to experience a nagging pain in her stomach she ignores it for some time and doesn't even mention it to Oliver. It's not going away, though, so she decides to go to the family doctor. Because Jane trivialises the pain the doctor doesn't take it too seriously and gives her a prescription for painkillers, suggesting that she return for a further consultation if the pain continues.

Jane gets only minimal relief from the tablets. She goes back to the doctor who arranges for her to go to hospital for tests. At this stage, she feels she has to tell Oliver, who is worried but convinces himself that because Jane has always seemed indestructible the tests won't show anything serious.

Oliver's optimism proves to be unfounded. Jane is riddled with cancer. The medical prognosis is that she has, at most, three months to live. And so it proves. The grief of the family knows no bounds as Jane's body gives up the struggle and they are left helplessly wondering how they're going to manage without her.

Jane herself was devastated. She tried to hold on but even her powerful will had no chance against the cancer. When she leaves her body she's in a state of utter distress at being separated from her family and also carries the burden of their overwhelming sadness. She's around them all the time but they're so numbed by their grief that they're not aware of her. She sees Oliver doing his best to organise things so that life can go on in some fashion for the family.

Jane is another of my 'charges'. I know that there's no point in trying to reach her while she's so enmeshed in her own grief and that of her family. In your time we're talking about an interval of nearly a year before Jane is ready to come to terms, even to a minor extent, with her new state. She has begun to relax a little as she sees that Olivier and the children have found a way of coping. She's had many bouts of exasperation because she's not there to sort things out when they get into a muddle, as they often do, and, no matter how hard she tries, she can't get through to any of them. However, they manage somehow to get by.

I have enlisted the help of Jane's father, Daniel, who had died when Jane was only fifteen. They had loved each other very much. As Jane begins to relax she becomes aware of her father. She's overjoyed to see him and they have a loving reunion. He talks to her and persuades her to go with him, constantly reassuring her that she'll continue to be able to be around her family.

We have arrived at a minor breakthrough. With the help of Daniel and other souls I'm able to show Jane that she can mind her family much more effectively by letting them go to some extent. We illustrate to her that her unbroken presence with the family is confusing them because it sets up a vibration around them which they don't understand. It's a heavy vibration caused by her distress at her separation from them and inability to be physically there to take care of them and all the details involved in managing the household. We arrange for her to meet other parents who have had to leave their families in somewhat similar situations. They invite her to join them in a cooperative grouping whose aim is to be available to help the families they have left on earth, while finding ways to make progress in their own evolution. Soon she realises that she has immediate access to experts in all sorts of fields.

XIX
22 August

MFC: Jane's case is quite common. If she could only have seen soon after her transition that she wasn't helping her family at all – rather the reverse – by staying around them without interruption in her state of distress and exasperation things would have been so much easier both for them and herself. She would still have had all the sadness of separation, and so would they, but she'd have been helped to realise very quickly that detaching from them to some extent didn't mean that she was abandoning them. The others in the group showed her very convincingly how well liaising arrangements which they had with their families' guides worked in practice.

> **PF**: *Is it usual for guides to operate in tandem with souls who pass on in, say, similar circumstances to Jane?*

MFC: It's becoming more so. I think it's an ideal arrangement. For example, Jane is introduced to the broad evolutionary picture involving herself and her family. She sees the purpose of the human tragedy in the context of what each of them set out to achieve through their lives on earth. She realises that she can meet them regularly while their bodies are asleep and talk to them and listen to them and hold them close. Usually they don't remember when they wake up or, if they do, they'll probably convince themselves that they were dreaming. Still, they're likely to find that things that were bothering them before they went to sleep seem to have sorted themselves out, if only because they have a different way of looking at them, and they feel much better.

Jane sometimes wishes that they would be more aware of her. At the same time, she understands that it's best that they get on with their lives and that, in due course, she'll be able to meet them again in a more conscious way for all of them. In the meantime, because she's looking down from her helicopter, as it were, and has a panoramic view, she's able to mind them in ways which wouldn't have been open to her on earth. And by getting on with her own life and releasing herself to the joy of her changed state she's spreading a loving vibration around her which includes her family in its embrace.

> **PF**: *The other side of the coin is where the human won't let go but continues to grieve for, say, a lost child, lover, parent or friend.*

MFC: Partings are an inevitable consequence of the temporary nature of the human condition, with death being seen as the final one. As we know, it's not (or what am I at?!). There are always good reasons for them in the context of overall evolutionary patterns.

What can I say? It's a matter of profound regret that the experience of humanness is still so painful for many souls. We can't interfere with free will. All we can do is try to lighten the burden of suffering to the best of our abilities. The more people accept that there's no final parting and that continuing contact between the physical and spirit states is possible, the more we hope and expect that the grief of separation will be lessened.

> **PF**: *When we look at the whole area of death and the grief that accrues to it I think it's fair to say that religions – at least Christian religions – haven't been very helpful. As far as I know, they would still be dismissive of the possibility, not to mention the desirability, of the sort of continuing contact we're discussing. And any idea of the validity of you communicating with me would surely be seen as a projection of my crazed imagination.*

MFC: Still, religions do provide comfort for many people. And, of course, it's central to religious teaching that life continues after death. Even the notion of eternal damnation in Hell can be put into the context of tormented states of mind, as we saw in the case of Alfredo; in such a state a moment is an eternity.

Fear and obedience to authority were very much the base of religious tradition as perceived by many of its adherents, but that's changing. Except where extreme fundamentalism is concerned, a positive approach tends to be emphasised more than a negative one; in other words, compassion, tolerance and love rather than fear.

All the same, I'd say that you'd be on to a good thing if you were to bet against our communications being received with open arms – not to mention open minds – by religious orthodoxy. What's new?

XX
24 August

PF: *Is it time to move on to your social commentary, which you promised, or do you want to discuss something else?*

MFC: There's no time like the present, if I may use a cliché which makes great sense where the world of spirit is concerned.

Things have advanced a lot since I was around in physical form. A century is nothing in terms of eternity, but the twentieth century, above all others, has been hugely significant for your planet. The technological miracles that have taken place would have been way beyond the wildest imaginings of Margaret or any of her contemporaries.

PF: *Is that a positive development, do you think?*

MFC: Of course it is. Would you have people go back to the drudgery of the last century or the early part of this one? What wouldn't people of those times have given for the labour saving devices of today?

PF: *When I started working in the Civil Service, we didn't even have photocopiers, not to mention computers. I didn't see television until I was in my twenties. The whole world of communications has opened up to an extraordinary degree in my lifetime. The possibilities for the next century are mind boggling.*

XXI
25 August

PF: *I didn't give you a chance to continue with the dialogue yesterday. I hope it's okay to go ahead now.*

MFC: It was blindingly obvious to me that there was no point in trying to preach spirituality at people who were on the edge of starvation and whose living conditions generally were atrocious. Conditions have much improved since my day in many parts of the world but, regrettably, there's still a long way to go.

PF: *People often rail at God for allowing so many injustices and atrocities to take place. Did you, when you were Margaret?*

MFC: I didn't rail, as you put it, but I prayed and then got on with whatever occurred to me. I believed that God was working through me and anybody else who wanted to help improve people's conditions. That's still my position except that I have a different perception of God, as I explained earlier in our dialogue.

PF: *In my experience some people are receptive, often enthusiastically, to the idea that they chose to be born and also chose the environment into which they felt it was desirable for them to be born. Others find it hard, if not impossible, to accept that they would have done so. Still others can't accept that souls would choose to incarnate, or reincarnate, into an environment of extreme poverty, barbarity and total disrespect for human rights.*

I have gone into all this elsewhere and the answers I have received make sense to me.

I feel, though, that people would like to hear your views.

It could be argued that, if it's a soul's purpose to be born into a situation of deprivation, then, say, a social reformer, as you were, could be frustrating that purpose and hindering rather than helping the soul in its spiritual quest.

MFC: As you'd expect, free will is at the heart of our consideration of these questions. Humans generally have been conditioned to an ambiguous view of free will. On the one hand, they're told that they have it; on the other hand, they're also told that it's subject to divine laws. But to be free is to be without conditions or limitations.

It's easy to see how confusion arises. Democratic societies subscribe to a philosophy that people are free to live their lives as they choose. Yet, those same societies enact laws which, if broken, lead to punishment, often by imprisonment. So, then, there's free will in theory but subject to conditions in practice.

There are frequent proclamations to the effect that what's neatly called the rule of law must prevail so that people can live together peaceably. New laws are framed, existing laws are amended or annulled according to politicians' perceptions of predominant public moods.

PF: *Doesn't all that add up to the people saying that they choose to exercise their free will by having such laws enacted on their behalf?*

MFC: It would if you had one hundred per cent agreement. Otherwise you have imposition of will by one group on another.

However, may we leave all that argument aside for the present? What I'm trying to explain is how people automatically regard themselves as having free will up to a point only. It seems logical to assume that the same thing applies in spirit realms.

You may remember that I talked earlier about the challenge of freedom. People expect to be regulated because they don't know anything else. Souls in spirit, on the other hand, are being guided towards coming to terms with existence in a dimension where there's no regulation.

It just can't be that a soul doesn't have total freedom of choice about whether to incarnate or reincarnate, or the environment into which to be born. Anything else would be a restriction on its free will, its divine nature, which knows no limitation. In its exercise of free will it may, of course, seek guidance, which is readily available.

Perhaps I could shed more light on this whole question of choice, etc., by giving you an illustration of how it works in practice.

Back in the middle ages, somewhere in Europe a boy whom I'm calling Cyprian – not his real name – was born. He was an intelligent boy and was particularly agile in discussion and debate. It was no surprise when he gravitated to the Church and, in due course, became a bishop.

He liked power and he used it to his own advantage. He had no doubts about his intellectual capacity and, in his view, he had no equal. He lived sumptuously and didn't deny himself in any aspect of life. There was no question of celibacy as far as he was concerned. Women were there to be used and discarded at his pleasure without any regard for their feelings. Because of his position and reputation nobody dared say no to him; those who had done so early on in his 'reign' were harshly punished, often fatally.

They were cruel times. People's free will didn't count for much. Inquisitional proceedings were widespread, with Cyprian as an ardent supporter. He wrote cleverly argued dissertations in favour of the most severe punishments for those who were accused of heretical practices or leanings – and they were many. It was an easy way to dispose of any unwanted relatives or potential rivals or nonconformists.

Cyprian's fame spread, bringing him favourable notice in papal circles, with resultant promotion to Archbishop and, later, Cardinal. With the expansion of his area of influence came increased power, with correspondingly greater scope for satisfying his indiscriminate voraciousness.

He ruled for many years with no lessening of his abuse of power. The only thing he couldn't control was his own mortality and eventually he succumbed to it. Many lavish tributes were paid to him on his death, and he was acclaimed as a saint.

There was no miraculous transformation on his transition. He carried his arrogance with him and changing awareness was a slow process for him. Eventually, however, he allowed himself to be helped and he came to some understanding of the extent of his abuse of power. There was no condemnation other than from himself.

It was a difficult stage for him. He decided that he would have to make reparation to the victims of his abuse and he sought guidance as to how he could do so. Various options, including reincarnation, were presented to him. It was stressed that there was no compulsion on him to choose any of the options, that indeed he didn't need to, but that he would be helped to put into operation any choice he made.

The upshot of all his considerations was that he chose to be born as a female child into an impoverished African environment. The reason why he chose to be female was because of his sexual abuses of many women, and he wanted to be able to experience in some way the pain that he had caused them. Remember that it's the soul's journey – the gender is incidental.

In that lifetime s/he experienced the ravages of poverty, internecine warfare and multiple rapes. There were many times when s/he wished for death, but it was slow in coming. Finally it did, as a result of one more brutal rape.

> **PF**: *Is it fair to draw general conclusions from that illustration? Cyprian abused power in extreme ways, including rape. In order to compensate for that he chose a lifetime where he knew he would be a victim of utter degradation and brutal abuse. If I'm an abuser – in whatever form – in one life am I likely to choose to be a victim in another?*

MFC: There's no hard and fast rule; in fact, as I keep saying, there are no rules at all in spirit. One of the choices that Cyprian had, in his perception of his situation, was to find ways to make reparation to each of his victims individually. But there were so many of them that it would have been a completely unrealistic option. Yet, he asked himself how could he ever forgive himself if he couldn't somehow share the suffering which he had imposed on his victims. Ultimately he chose what seemed to him the best way to do that. After his transition from the later life he was able to begin the process of forgiving himself.

You see, the ultimate 'sin' is betrayal of our divine natures, love. We've all 'sinned' in that way – all of us who have been through the earth experience and some who haven't. We can only restore ourselves fully to the expression of our divine natures when we forgive ourselves completely for our betrayal.

> **PF**: *May I bring you back to what I was postulating earlier about a social reformer interfering with a soul's chosen purpose? Suppose, for example, that somebody like you were, or a relief organisation, came along and changed completely the conditions under which the reincarnated Cyprian was existing, wouldn't that have thwarted what s/he was trying to achieve? Would it have involved choosing to have another go?*

MFC: Divine – unconditional – love does not require souls to go on punishing themselves for their betrayals. That's their own choice. The conditions of hardship which obtain on earth would cease to exist if souls didn't go on punishing themselves, and, in the process, others, for their acts of unawareness. Therefore, the more that can be done by individuals or by groups to help to raise awareness the quicker that objective will be reached.

XXII
26 August

PF: *So — the sources of pain and suffering are there because of our abuse of free will. The more we raise our awareness levels and help others to do so the less abuse there will be. And the process of raising awareness is inevitably assisted by improvement in living conditions. Do you agree with those statements?*

MFC: Yes.

PF: *If I may go back to Cyprian again for a minute, there's something I'd like to clarify. Suppose that people's awareness levels were raised to such an extent that there would be no conditions of deprivation and abuse how would he manage to purge himself of his guilt?*

MFC: He didn't have to choose to be a victim. He made that choice because he considered that it was the only appropriate way he could make reparation; the punishment fitting the crime type of thing.

The notion of punishment has been so much a part of human conditioning for so long that it's very hard to get rid of it. It's fascinating to see the reaction of souls (after they have left their physical bodies and adjusted to the spirit state) when they realise that punishment doesn't fit into the scheme of things in spirit at all. More often than not there's a mixture of shock, incredulity, surprise, and then exhilaration.

PF: *In Cyprian's case, when he realised that no heavenly judge was going to punish him, couldn't he just have said 'well, that's fine', or words to that effect, and got on with his new life without bothering about making reparation?*

MFC: It was open to him to do so. However, he couldn't – I mean he found it impossible to do so. How can I explain? Imagine a huge room which is brilliantly lit by hundreds of incandescent bulbs. One by one the bulbs are dimmed until the room is in darkness.

Let's say that the soul Cyprian is the room in all its shining brightness. As he betrayed his divine nature over and over again he dimmed the lights bit by bit. He had taken away his capacity to see. Once he realised what he had done he wanted to be able to see as he had done originally, which meant restoring the room to its former brightness.

I used the rough analogy of the room because I wanted to show that there was an easier way towards 'redemption' than that chosen by Cyprian. How could he restore the room to its former brightness? Simply by pressing a switch. The switch is self-forgiveness for his unawareness in his human state.

> **PF**: *I can imagine all sorts of objections to that as being far too easy. Wouldn't there be an outcry from all his victims at him getting off scot-free like that? Are you saying that all somebody who might have committed the most heinous crimes against humanity need do is forgive himself and that takes care of everything for him?*

MFC: Before he could get round to forgiving himself he'd have to understand what he was forgiving himself for. The extent of his blindness would be apparent to him before he could restore his sight. He'd have reached a stage where he'd be incapable of committing any of those crimes again.

> **PF**: *There's an old saying to the effect that to understand all is to forgive all. Is that what you mean?*

MFC: Exactly. When a soul reaches the stage of being open to see the film of its complete evolution to date it can observe all its ups and downs, its acts of cruelty and compassion, its expressions of hate and love; like a seesaw, always struggling for balance and never succeeding. When it had a life as an abuser it was likely to have sought to balance it by being a victim in another life on a scale equal to that of the abuse in so far as that could be estimated; in the long run, a never ending cycle of repetition going nowhere.

PF: *Are you saying that, for example, Cyprian's life as a female victim was a futile exercise?*

MFC: He wanted to punish himself and it fulfilled that purpose. Having done that, which to him was an act of atonement, he felt better.

If we look at the life from that perspective it wasn't futile. However, from the point of view of growth in awareness, it was. It was essentially an act of self-indulgence and, again, an offence against his divine nature. That sounds rather heavy and perhaps surprising, but it's important to understand that, whether as an abuser or a victim, I'm out of step with my divine nature. So what I need to do is to forgive myself for making a choice to be either. That's the key to breaking the repetitive pattern of cause and effect – indeed to obviating any perceived need for further reincarnation.

PF: *What you're saying seems to me to be tremendously significant. My understanding of it is that we are inadvertently contributing to the continuing patterns of violence, etc., by choosing to be victims in order to make up for previous abuses on our part. If we didn't make those choices there would be no victims and therefore no scope for abusers. By being victims we're providing avenues for our abusers to choose to be victims later, and so on ad infinitum.*

MFC: That's it.

PF: *But suppose that before I reincarnated I chose to be a victim and having heard what you have to say I decide that I don't want to be a victim any more, what can I do?*

MFC: You've said it – you decide not to be a victim any more. A reminder – you create your reality from within. As you think, so you are.

PF: *As simple as that.*

MFC: Everything in spirit is simple. We're trying to bring similar simplicity into human consciousness.

When we – and by 'we' I mean every soul who has ever taken on a physical body – examine the history of our evolution we soon see that we could never make adequate reparation for our abuse of our divine natures no matter how much we might choose to punish ourselves. When we come to an acceptance of that and admit to ourselves that we expressed our free will idiotically, that we regret what we did, but that we can't turn the clock back, we reach a haven of understanding that, mercifully, we can release ourselves to the fullness of divine love in us by forgiving ourselves.

XXIII
27 August

PF: *Ideally, I decide that I don't want to be an abuser any more, either.*

MFC: Yes. Neither an abuser nor a victim be!

PF: *I mightn't know, though, when I am. It can be a subtle, manipulative thing.*

MFC: You'll have created an awareness in yourself. If you fail it's not likely to be in a major way. All you can do is your best.

PF: *When you talk about there being no laws or rules or regulations in spirit and, incidentally, no concept of punishment, people would very likely find it hard to imagine how things could be similarly arranged on earth. In spirit you don't have to bother about money or religion or nationalism, the sort of things that people fight about or even kill for. I seem to be getting an impression from you that you'd like to see the way of spirit mirrored on earth in the management of all its affairs.*

MFC: Not just me – many of us are focused on that, including your friend, Shebaka, as you know. Putting it simply, we'd like people to be able to enjoy themselves more than they do at present. We know that a way to achieve that would be to create conditions where there would be no need for laws and punishments.

On the subject of punishment, if you cast you mind back to when you were going to school, corporal punishment was the order of the day then, wasn't it?

PF: *Emphatically and often brutally so.*

MFC: And it isn't now. The system of education hasn't collapsed because of that change, has it? In fact, it's incomparably better. Teachers don't have to be abusers, nor children victims, as was so often the case. I think we can agree that punishment and the fear it generated never brought out the best in children. It's hardly likely to do so with adults either. After all, what are adults but big children?

XXIV
29 August

PF: *I took a break from our discussions yesterday because I wanted to get a clearer understanding of what has come up in the last few sessions. I hope you don't mind if I recap a little.*

If I'm correct, what you're saying is that the human condition itself with all it ramifications is explainable in terms of abusers and victims. All people have been abusers at different stages in their evolution and, as balancing efforts, have chosen to be victims repeatedly.

MFC: Yes.

PF: *While it would be wonderful if people in the exercise of their free will did not become abusers the most vitally important thing is that souls should choose not to be victims, since abusers can't function without victims. All souls need to do is to use their free will to decide not to be victims any more; but that 'all' involves reaching an understanding of the whole evolutionary process and their place in it. That's the crunch then, isn't it?*

MFC: So it is.

PF: *And, of course, if there were no abusers and no victims there wouldn't be any need for laws and punishment, would there? Certainly not criminal laws.*

And if there were no perceived need on their part for souls to reincarnate would that mean that the population of the planet would be set on a diminishing pattern according as souls choose not to be victims any more?

MFC: The planet could become a sort of divine playground, another dimension in which souls could express fully the joy of being.

> **PF**: *My teasing all this out must seem tortuous to you as we've been over it all already. But to use what I think is an awful 'in' expression, I want to get my head round it all, and not risk any misunderstanding of what you're communicating.*
>
> *It seems a harsh thing to say to people who are victims of what may seem to them to be cruel fate that their situation is a consequence of their own choice.*

MFC: It is a harsh reality – a temporary one, mercifully. As I see it, there are three ways of looking at their situation. They're in it

(a) as a result of their own free will; or
(b) because God, or some such Supreme Being, wills it to be so; or
(c) because life on earth is an arbitrary coming together of circumstances with no rhyme or reason to them, and when it's over, it's over – there's nothing beyond it.

We had better dismiss the third option – or we've been wasting a lot of energy!

The first two options are really one and the same. They would only be different if there was a separation between God and souls. If you like, we can say that God gave free will to all souls, but we all continued to be part of God, so that, ideally, in expressing our free will we're fully expressing our divinity

We're back again to our understanding of free will. There's no other answer I can give you except that it's their own free will in action.

> **PF**: *It sounds uncaring, though. It's like saying to somebody in a dire situation – 'you've made your bed, now you can lie in it.*

MFC: It's only the initial perception that makes it seem hard. No matter how difficult my situation is, once I accept that nobody else but myself is responsible for it, then I have shaken off the shackles of crying out at God or cruel fate or the government or an individual or individuals. I can then allow myself to be helped to help myself.

PF: *And that's where guides and all the social reformers, etc., come in.*

MFC: That's how divine love expresses itself. It's not into blaming or judging or punishing people. Its only concern is to help souls get back to the full, joyful expression of their divinity.

PF: *In Cyprian's case, as you said, it was explained to him that he didn't need to reincarnate as a victim. Why wasn't that enough for him?*

MFC: Because he was so racked with guilt over his abuse of his free will that he felt that he owed it to his victims to punish himself in an extreme way.

PF: *But that didn't help them at all, did it?*

MFC: Of course not. But, as I said, it helped him to feel better. Much as they regretted his choice those who were helping him on this side couldn't stop him exercising it; that would have been an interference with his free will.

PF: *It must be a strangely ironic experience for us when we look back over our evolutionary journeys to realise that we kept on repeatedly putting ourselves through totally unnecessary trials and tribulations.*

MFC: The human tragi-comedy. You don't even have to wait to do that – just look back at the present life. It's on a vastly smaller scale, but you can see the pattern.

PF: *May I back pedal a little bit, please? Is there an implication in what we've been discussing that all victims without exception, even those who suffer through illness, disability, poverty, or any conceivable source of deprivation, have chosen such conditions in order to compensate for acts of abuse on their part in other lives?*

MFC: There's more than an implication. That's what I'm saying. But look at it this way. Everybody who has ever gone through the earth experience has abused free will. The planet was designed to help souls to free themselves from the consequences of that abuse. So nobody is exempt and nobody need feel that he or she has committed especially heinous crimes because they find themselves in difficult circumstances at present. They have probably chosen to be excessively hard on themselves. People do, don't they?

PF: *Some do, certainly. What about Jesus – was he a victim?*

MFC: Of course he was. Why he chose to be is a different matter.

It's obviously not wise to make any judgements about individuals or draw conclusions from their particular circumstances. The reasons why souls choose to be victims are as distinctive as the individuals themselves. Some souls may choose to take on the burden of being victims in order to help others by their example. That doesn't mean that they're not seeking to compensate for abuse of free will on their part at an earlier stage in their evolution.

PF: *What does social reform mean to you now?*

MFC: Social reform in the sense of improved living conditions for everybody is the end result of raising awareness all round. That means more emphasis on education. That was one of my 'babies' when I was last on earth.

Primarily I see education as a means of helping people to open their minds – not a collection of facts, obviously, but a way of thinking. The teachers need to be educated as well as the students.

PF: *I know I'm digressing, but I want to ask this now in case I forget it later. How is it that, given that they have incarnated or reincarnated from a spirit state, some people believe that there's nothing beyond physical existence?*

MFC: You're not digressing really because the answer comes into the sphere of education, as I see it. As you know, the broad picture is that the soul gets a fresh chance without the encumbrance of remembering previous existence with its incidental traumas. After that, it becomes a question of individual choice of parents, environment, etc.,. It depends on what a soul has set out to achieve in a particular earth life.

Suppose, for example, you had been a fanatical devotee of a specific religious organisation and, not alone did you refuse to tolerate any other belief, but you actively persecuted those who did. You might reasonably choose not to have anything to do with religion in a later life with the aim of freeing yourself from your previous obsession.

Then suppose that something, a book you read, say, or a meeting with somebody, presents you with a philosophy of openness and tolerance that appeals to you. You may be receptive to it in a way that you'd never have countenanced in your previous life.

Alternatively, maybe you just live out your life as an agnostic or an atheist. You'll probably get a bit of a surprise when you pass on; that, in itself, should be enough to promote some curiosity about your unexpected condition.

XXV
30 August

PF: *When you talk about teachers needing to be educated what do you mean?*

MFC: I don't mean to cast a reflection on teachers in any way. I'm well aware of the marvellous work they do. As I'll explain, I'm not thinking of teaching in an exclusively vocational sense.

My perspective is based on what we on this side see as important towards raising people's awareness. We want to accelerate the whole process so that souls won't continue to be caught in the web of repeating patterns of cause and effect that we've been discussing. Apart from our work as guides generally, we have been focusing in particular on the elimination of the perceived need for what I might call 'victimhood'. To this end we'd like to have considerably expanded cooperative arrangements with souls who are at present in physical bodies.

It would break your heart if you saw the state of confusion that many – far from all, thankfully, - souls are in when they make the transition from their physical state. Either they're expecting to be, as it were, put into 'bad boxes' and sent to unimaginable places of punishment, or they have no idea at all what to expect. With souls who are in one or other of those categories progress is inevitably very slow as far as we are concerned. When we manage to get through to them eventually we're handicapped by the fact that we're all in spirit. I know that may sound strange to you. What I mean is that, because what they perceive as their crimes or sins or shortcomings of whatever kind happened on earth, then, once they become aware of the possibility of reincarnation, they are likely to convince themselves that the best place for atonement is back on earth. Not all of them, but a sizeable proportion; one is too many, in my view.

PF: *You don't seem to be too keen on reincarnation as a means of growth, are you?*

MFC: Looked at from the growth end, I don't think it has been particularly effective so far. The fly in the ointment is how people use their free will. 'You can lead a horse to water………' type of thing.

On the other hand, if reincarnation wasn't a possibility we'd have a much harder task in trying to get through to souls who are caught in guilt traps. On balance, it's worth the pain and hassle of a life as a victim if the soul will then feel more free (having done its self-imposed penance) to open itself to enjoying its life in spirit.

My barometer of the success or failure of reincarnation as a process has to be the levels of pain and suffering on earth. The more that those levels diminish, the happier I am with the process.

What we're aiming for is that reincarnation will be seen as a joyful adventure rather than a via dolorosa.

I'm seeing education as something which isn't confined to schools or colleges or a means whereby people obtain various kinds of qualifications which enhance their career prospects. All that's fine. What I'm thinking about, though, is a process which continues all through people's lives and, ideally, provides them with a philosophy that gives them an understanding of themselves and their place in the universal scheme of things. All the academic qualifications in the world won't be of any use to them when they leave their bodies, as they surely will, if they don't have such an understanding.

Everybody is a teacher and everybody is a student. People are constantly teaching, and learning from, each other. Some operate on more public platforms than others – such as professional teachers, writers, media pundits, counsellors. Many highly effective teachers have no formal qualifications at all.

XXVI
1 September

PF: *You've indicated that in order to help themselves to decide not be victims any more souls need to reach an understanding of the whole evolutionary process and their place in it. You've already dwelt on this, but I hope you don't mind if we discuss it a little further.*

I'm here on earth. I don't have access to the film of my evolution, so that I can't see in technicolor, so to speak, how impossible it would be for me to make reparation to all the victims of my abuse of them no matter how many times I might choose to be a victim myself. While I'm still in a physical body how can I reach the required level of understanding?

MFC: The first and most important point is acceptance of your own divinity. To an orthodox religious practitioner that may sound sacrilegious. However it sounds, the fact is that all souls are part of God; in other words, the loving energy that is God animates all souls. So in accepting your divinity you're not setting yourself above – or below – anybody else.

How do you know whether what I'm saying is true, particularly when it seems to be contrary to so much religious teaching? You haven't any proof, that's for sure, any more than you have proof that I'm who I say I am or even that I'm there at all.

PF: *As far as I personally am concerned I don't have any doubts, certainly not about the divinity part nor even about you being you, if you know what I mean, and you communicating with me, in spite of my having raised questions about that earlier in our dialogue. I wouldn't have persevered with this book if I had any continuing doubts. But my certainty isn't much help to any reader.*

MFC: May I repeat my question – how do you know, when you haven't any physical evidence?

PF: *I just know. That's the only answer I can give.*

MFC: That's it – a knowing that reaches beyond all analysis. It comes when people are ready. It's as if a light inside them has been switched on. It's no different in spirit, which people might find surprising. The closed mind works equally effectively in that state – as does the open one. All the proof you'll ever need is in that knowing; and, in fact, it's all the proof you'll ever get. Admittedly I have an advantage over you in that I can see you and you can't see me, except vaguely sometimes, as you said, so that you have to take me more on trust than I you. But when it comes to seeing God we're both in the same boat – we're seeing God around us all the time in every soul with whom we come into contact.

PF: *That can be a bit of a challenge sometimes.*

MFC: Don't I know! I wouldn't have been much inclined to see God in most of the bishops I met.

PF: *Have you come across them subsequently?*

MFC: Yes. We've been able to laugh about our 'tete-a-tetes'. I haven't seen much of them. I felt I had to acknowledge that they helped me fulfil my purpose, although I didn't think so at the time, so I thanked them and left them to their own explorations.

Once you accept your divinity, the next step is to align yourself with it as much as you can. If you like, you can take an easy route with that by asking your guides to help you with it. They're helping you anyway, but when you're consciously cooperating with them you're using your free will in your best spiritual interests. It's no big deal; all you need do is send a thought to them and they'll pick it up. They'll help you with everything, no matter what it is. You'll find that you'll be guided to the people, the books, etc., that will be stepping stones on your way to the understanding you need.

XXVII
2 September

PF: *(I'm at Gatwick Airport, London, having left Dublin this morning. I'm waiting for a connecting flight to San Diego, California. With all the milling crowds through the airport I have plenty of opportunity to see some of God's variety of expression.)*

Suppose I don't want to bother with guides, that I'd rather work things out under my own steam, have you any helpful suggestions?

MFC: Is there an implication that I might make unhelpful suggestions?!

Of course that would be your own choice. I assume your question is hypothetical unless it's an indirect way of sacking me!

Our role as guides is to help souls to connect more fully with their own divinity. Meditation can be helpful in that context – it is anyway, whether you're using your guides or not. As long as your intention is to allow yourself to flow more and more with your divine energy it doesn't much matter what form of meditation you use, nor do you need to set up any ritual around it; do, if you like, of course.

I must do the public relations bit, though! Suppose you're due to travel to a location which is, say, fifty miles (or its equivalent) from your present one. You have only two choices – either you take a bus or a train or you walk. Which would you choose? You'll get there either way, but the journey will certainly take much longer if you walk and your feet, and probably other parts of you, are likely to be sore. Guides, like the bus or the train, would help to take the weight off your feet, in a manner of speaking.

PF: *(As I write this I'm literally up in the air, flying to San Diego.)*

Why do we usually refer to the world of spirit as being 'up there'? Up here in mid-air am I closer to that world? If the plane crashes I certainly will be!

MFC: It's logical enough. To be light as air is a common expression. In spirit we're in a lighter vibration than that of earth. We're not controlled by gravity like you are. Showing wings on angels is symbolically a way of illustrating the freedom and lightness of spirit.

By the way, I'll make sure the plane won't crash even if I have to hold up the wings myself! What a difference it would have made to me in my Margaret days if I could have travelled like you're doing now.

PF: *You could always change your mind and come back again.*

MFC: I can travel all I want as I am – and it's free. Seriously though, I won't change my mind. I feel that I can play a more significant part in helping to raise consciousness by staying put. I don't mean that to be taken generally – I'm just speaking for myself.

PF: *When we were discussing proof and you said that inner knowing was all the proof we're ever going to get I was surprised at first, but then I realised that, of course, that's the way it has to be. So, going through all sorts of contortions searching for proof is a waste of energy.*

MFC: I agree. You can go to the ends of the earth searching for proof and you won't find it.

XXVIII
5 September

MFC: Coming to accept that the proof you're looking for, if you are, is in your moment by moment being, and how you experience that, relieves you of a huge burden, essentially of fear, and helps you enjoy each moment spontaneously.

> **PF**: *I understand that. Thanks.*
>
> *Suppose there's somebody who's continually depressed and has tried every therapy, etc., that has come to his attention, but with only minimal success; do you have any suggestions as to how he might be cured.*

MFC: At the very least I can say that I understand depression because I suffered from it, most recently as Margaret. The break up of the family home, Charles's death, and my father's not long afterwards, were all deeply depressing experiences for me. And all that was before I had the dubious pleasure of getting into bed with bishops – metaphorically speaking, of course!

I gave in to the depression, I was sad, angry, even bitter at times, but in the final analysis I just got on with life as best I could.

Unfortunately, bouts of depression are part of the human experience. We're trying to change all that and we're succeeding, but more slowly than we'd like.

The primary source of depression is the free will choice of souls to be victims as their way of atoning for earlier 'sins' on their part. They carry with them into their new incarnations subconscious emotional baggage, which spills out, and often overwhelms them, without warning, sabotaging any chance they may have of feeling good about themselves. As we eliminate 'victimhood' we'll eliminate depression.

Because people suffer from a carryover of subconscious guilt they feel that they don't deserve to be happy and, since they're used to it, that feeling is, ironically, often a source of comfort. The perceived impossibility of being happy without pain being round the corner seems to make it easier to continue to be miserable. At least that's a familiar condition.

> ***PF:*** *Eliminating 'victimhood', while it's the ideal solution, would seem to be a long term one, in a general sense at least. Suppose, though, that my hypothetical depressive doesn't have any time for reincarnation and is contemptuous of the idea that he might have chosen to be a victim, how can I help him?*

MFC: If you refer back to my story about Johann you'll remember that the method I adopted was to sit with him, and listen when he was ready to talk. Patience and non-judgementalism were the key ingredients. In due course the group took over from me.

There's no pat answer to your question really. First of all, you need to accept that you may not be able to help him at all because he may continue to close himself off from being helped. You can share your philosophy of life with him and something of it may reach him – but be prepared for it not to. The idea of having his own special guides or guardian angels might appeal to him, or it might seem like utter rubbish to him. As you play the situation by ear – with the help of your guides, I would suggest, – he may begin to let go, if you're patient enough, but if you can't get through to him despite all your efforts, don't worry – he'll come round eventually. In any case it wouldn't be advisable to join him in his depression – which is easy enough to do if you start agonising over your seeming failure to help him.

XXIX
6 September

MFC: All forms of healing, whether of depression or any condition, operate from within. Those who don't want to be healed won't be until they do – it's as simple as that.

> **PF**: *If I were to say to my hypothetical depressive that he's that because he wants to be, I'd be met with an outcry. Put mildly, the question might be – 'Who would want to suffer like that?'*

MFC: And of course he would feel completely justified in his reaction. But yet, even though he may not believe in anything beyond his human existence, it's still a fact that he, as soul, will have chosen to be a victim. If a soul is hell-bent, in a manner of speaking, on self-punishment, all we can do is to be patient, as I've said already. The old saying that we're our own worst enemies is indisputably true, as I can now see in a far more comprehensive way than would have been possible for me on earth.

> **PF**: *Animals figure prominently on earth. Do you have any comments about them?*

MFC: They are soul. All souls are part of God. That's it really. It follows that it's important that they are treated with respect and love.

> **PF**: *You weren't vegetarian, were you?*

MFC: No.

> **PF**: *Would you be, supposing you were to change your mind and reincarnate?*

MFC: I'd be inclined to be, but I probably wouldn't.

All human forms are just vehicles for growth in awareness. Picture them all linked together as in a chain, with the human state being at the end of the chain. Each link in the chain is supporting every other link; the others are moving towards being absorbed into the human state. Until they're ready to do so it's helpful for them to have human survival so that, ideally, the humans will progress significantly in their evolution, which in turn will help all the other links in the chain.

I can tell you that if I were to reincarnate I'd be campaigning actively for animal rights. The fact that there's so much cruelty to animals is a festering wound in human consciousness. Fortunately there are many people who are working wonders in creating shifts in awareness where animals are concerned. Needless to say, we on this side are helping them in every way we can.

I have seen many loving reunions of pets with their former owners. These are often totally unexpected and are all the more joyful for that.

XXX
17 September

PF: *(Waiting at San Diego Airport to fly back to Dublin via London.)*

I can't think of anything else to ask you at present so I'll have to leave it up to you if there's more you want to say.

MFC: May I turn tables on you and ask you some questions? How do you feel about what I have transmitted to you?

PF: *Happy. Your experience and descriptions of life after death are very comforting.*

MFC: My experience was very comforting for me too, I can assure you. Do you wish to highlight anything else in the communications?

PF: *I hadn't thought of the interaction between abuse and 'victimhood' in the way you explained it. That has been most enlightening for me.*

MFC: Does it make sense to you?

PF: *Totally. It explains in a very simple way how we have allowed ourselves to become prisoners of our free will instead of enjoying it as the wonderful gift that it is.*

MFC: As you know, prisoners who are released after long prison sentences more often than not find it very difficult to adjust to the relative freedom of the outside world. The routine of institutional life, much though they may have felt trapped by it, had become the only form of freedom they knew. I mentioned the challenge of freedom earlier. How to be free spirits – that's what all souls are faced with. The main purpose of this dialogue, as far as I'm concerned, is to help people to meet that challenge.

XXXI
20 September

PF: *You have made some observations through earlier sessions dealing with social reform. With the benefit of all your experience and your level of awareness how would you reorganise the planet to help bring about conditions that you would regard as ideal?*

MFC: I was waiting for that question – well, I have to admit I inspired it – and I'm delighted to have the opportunity to answer it now.

I'd make a movie based on how things are arranged in spirit. I'd include examples, like the stories of Johann and the others I outlined earlier, showing them on earth and then later in spirit. I'd also show how we work as guides, both individually (e.g., with Monica) and collectively (e.g., in committees or groups). The three part story of Catherine and Stephen would illustrate the painful, yet finally triumphant, progress of love through a spread of centuries.

As I've already mentioned, we have no hierarchical systems. My movie would show a model society in operation where all administrative matters would be handled by people working together along the lines of our committee systems. (It would be superfluous of me to go into detail on this, as I'd only be repeating what is outlined comprehensively in Part 11 of THE GRAND DESIGN IV.)

My movie would be produced in such a way as to give audiences a feeling of participation in it. Your films as they are generally produced at present show action on a screen with the audience facing the screen as spectators – rather like stage plays with their distinctly separate auditoriums and frontal raised platforms. Technological developments are already moving towards bringing the screen around the audience, as it were, - as you saw in an IMAX cinema in San

Diego. My movie would go further in that direction, involving audiences without threatening them in any way. My hope would be that the movie would reach people in ways which would help their growth in awareness, inspire them to be free spirits and encourage them to emulate what they would have seen on screen – the relevant question being – 'why not?'. Thus would the planet become an increasingly harmonious and joyful place.

PF: *But you won't be coming back to make your movie.*

MFC: No, but somebody else will do it – better than I could. I'll keep an eye on it, though!

PF: *When the utopian scheme of things is fully achieved, when there will be no more abuse and no more 'victimhood', how will you occupy yourself, given that so much of your attention is at present focused on helping others?*

MFC: I wish I could say that that state of affairs would be reached soon. My movie would have to make a phenomenal impact to allow me to start thinking about negotiating a redundancy package from my job as a guide! That's what I'd hope for, of course.

It's hard for you to imagine a state of doing nothing. For you doing has an end in mind. For me doing is like that sometimes, too, - for example, helping a 'trapped' soul to release itself. In the ultimate sense, being is also doing; in other words, I'll just be, and out of that state I'll do whatever I want to do. I won't need any help and no other soul will need my help. I'll be a bundle of fun and joyfulness! That's it in a nutshell.

XXXII
23 September

PF: *I'm excited by the idea of the movie. It seems to me that it could break down the barriers between the spirit and physical worlds in a way that's never been done. The effect on global consciousness would be enormous. Were you serious when you intimated that the movie would be made?*

MFC: I was never more serious. It will be made and shown widely. You may well ask how can I predict that with such certainty since a lot of people with the vagaries of their free will would be involved in such a project. I predict it because it's something that people agreed to work on before they reincarnated – in the same way as we agreed to record these discussions.

PF: *It looks like the next century is going to be an interesting one for the planet. I'm tempted to ask whether I'll be here to see the film, but I think I'm better off not knowing. I'd rather have the possibility of enjoying the wonder of how it might materialise. I'll see it anyway, one way or the other.*

It feels as if we're ready to wind up our dialogue, are we?

MFC: Yes.

PF: *I hope I haven't distorted in any way what you wanted to say.*

MFC: No. It's all there. I'm happy with the way you have interpreted and recorded what I have been conveying to you telepathically.

PF: *I'm grateful to you for the privilege of allowing me to collaborate* *with you on this book.*

MFC: It's as we agreed. My thanks to you, too.

I think it's appropriate for me to sign off with a loving, temporarily parting, wish for all – no more 'victimhood'.

ABOUT THE AUTHOR

Paddy McMahon was born in 1933 in County Clare in the west of Ireland, and has lived in Dublin since 1952. Employed in the Irish Civil Service from 1952 until 1988, he became aware that he and all people had spirit guides-guardian angels, and that we can communicate with them if we so choose. These communications began in 1978, and inspired him to become increasingly involved in spiritual counseling and lecturing. Paddy's first communications from the highly-evolved spiritual being Shebaka began in 1981.

BOOKS BY PADDY MCMAHON

There Are No Goodbyes:
Guided By Angels - My Tour of the Spirit World

Peacemonger:
More Dialogue with Margaret Anna Cusack

Living without Fear:
Dialogue with J. Krishnamurti

Amongst Equals:
More Dialogue with J. Krishnamurti

A Free Spirit:
Dialogue with Margaret Anna Cusack The Nun of Kenmare

The Joy of Being
Illustrations by Michel

The Grand Design:
Reflections of a soul / oversoul
Selected excerpts from the five volumes

The Grand Design – V:
Reflections of a soul / oversoul

The Grand Design – IV:
Reflections of a soul / oversoul

The Grand Design – III:
Reflections of a soul / oversoul

The Grand Design – II:
Reflections of a soul / oversoul

The Grand Design – I:
Reflections of a soul / oversoul

Printed in Great Britain
by Amazon